WORKING THE CRO
Social Media Marketin
for Business

Eileen remains on the cutting edge of social media strategy that when implemented returns a measurable return on interest. I would highly recommend her book to any business who wants to deepen their customer interactions through powerful word of mouth marketing strategies.

Kim Matlock
Senior Director, Digital & Consumer Related Marketing, Hard Rock International

Brown's varied experience and analysis of the needs of both small and large businesses for social media makes her advice stand out from the crowded field – and told in the lively voice those hearing her via social media channels have come to know and love.

Betsy Aoki
Senior Program Manager, Social Media, Microsoft

Eileen Brown blends extensive real world business experience with in-depth social media knowledge to create a unique and valuable guide.

Professor Sue Thomas
Institute of Creative Technologies, De Montfort University

It's a good book. If you don't have a social media strategy yet, then reading this one will take you a long way forward. I recommend it to any business wondering about 'the twitter'.

Kate Gregory's Blog

BCS, The Chartered Institute for IT
Our mission as BCS, The Chartered Institute for IT, is to enable the information society. We promote wider social and economic progress through the advancement of information technology science and practice. We bring together industry, academics, practitioners and government to share knowledge, promote new thinking, inform the design of new curricula, shape public policy and inform the public.

Our vision is to be a world-class organisation for IT. Our 70,000 strong membership includes practitioners, businesses, academics and students in the UK and internationally. We deliver a range of professional development tools for practitioners and employees. A leading IT qualification body, we offer a range of widely recognised qualifications.

Further Information
BCS The Chartered Institute for IT, First Floor, Block D, North Star House, North Star Avenue, Swindon, SN2 1FA, United Kingdom.
T +44 (0) 1793 417 424
F +44 (0) 1793 417 444
www.bcs.org/contactus

WORKING THE CROWD
Social Media Marketing for Business

Eileen Brown

Published by British Informatics Society Limited (BISL), a wholly owned subsidiary of BCS, The Chartered Institute for IT, First Floor, Block D, North Star House, North Star Avenue, Swindon, SN2 1FA, United Kingdom.
www.bcs.org

ISBN 978-906124-71-7

British Cataloguing in Publication Data.
A CIP catalogue record for this book is available at the British Library.

Typeset by Lapiz Digital Services, Chennai, India.
Printed at CPI Antony Rowe, Chippenham, UK.

This book is for my husband Steve, who keeps hold of the loop of my yo-yo string

CONTENTS

LIST OF FIGURES

AUTHOR

Eileen Brown is CEO of Amastra: a company which helps you achieve your aspirations using offline and online social methods. She has been in a variety of roles in the IT industry since 1993. After spending 10 years in the Merchant Navy as Shell Tankers' first female Deck Officer, Eileen managed a fleet of ships in a container shipping company, before moving to IT support, then training and management at a training provider in London, technical consultancy at HP and Manager of the IT Pro Evangelist team at Microsoft.

Eileen helps you achieve your goals using social media and Web 2.0 to find and engage with customers, identify your influencers and gain advocates for your brand. She works with you to improve perception about your brand and create a vibrant community, using Social Media to amplify your message and improve the quality of your connection to your customers to increase satisfaction.

She is an accomplished and well-known international speaker and expert on Social Media, Online Branding, Web 2.0 and Unified Communications and is a key advocate for the advancement of Women in Technology. She explores the art of the possible, looking at how technology is changing the world we live in, simplifying work and making staff more productive.

Eileen is a member of the IoD, the BCS, and a fellow of the RSA. She is part of the BCS Strategic panel for Women in IT, sits on the BCS Committee for the Essex region and is the Chair of the Intellect Women in Technology Committee. However, her life isn't spent entirely at her laptop. Away from work, she makes jam and chutney in awesome quantities, tends her flock of chickens, grows organic vegetables and fruit and races around the countryside in her home-built 6.6 litre cobra replica car. Whenever she encounters warmer waters, she scuba dives as much as possible to get away from the phone...

ACKNOWLEDGEMENTS

I'd like to thank all of the people who gave me feedback during the writing of the book and kept me on track as I started to wander. Kay Ewbank read through the chapters and told me how much I preferred commas to full stops in my sentences. Shorter sentences. Shorter sentences. Kate Burton talked to me about book structure and flow, and Mary Branscombe talked to me about vision. Matthew Flynn was very encouraging and patient throughout the process, answering my daft questions and explaining how the publishing process actually works. He also caught my fondness for the grocer's apostrophe at an early stage. Ian Murphy spent ages explaining how books are published and how to get over writer's block when it hits really hard. Betsy Aoki gave me some great tips about making the book more human so that it didn't read entirely like a textbook. Thanks, Betsy, for believing in me.

And Steve supplied me with food, wine and words of encouragement when I started to flag, and managed the running of my home life whilst I researched and wrote. Thank you all.

GLOSSARY

If you've never heard of social media, social networking or social marketing, here are a few of the main terms and phrases that I use throughout the book. I'll explain more of the terms as we move through the chapters, so this isn't an exhaustive list at all.

Aggregation   Software or a website that collects information from several sources for use in one place.

Application programming interface   Enables a software application to interact with other software programs.

Blog   An online chronological diary of entries written by a user or group of users and searchable online.

Folksonomy   The users of a site classify web page information in ways that are useful to them and do not necessarily use the formal taxonomy assigned by the web page designer.

Generation Y   People born between 1980 and 2000.

Hub   The centre of activity of a social group. This can be applied to personal relationships, or to a computer network device which connects multiple devices together to act as a single segment of the network.

Influencer   Anyone who has the ability to change people's perception about a concept, idea or product leading to a change in online behaviour and buying decisions.

Location aware applications   Applications on a mobile device that use the coordinates provided by the mobile network to locate the position of the device.

Mashup   An application on the web containing data from one or more sources which creates a new web service.

Microblogging   Creating a shortened form of a blog entry.

Online brand   Your online presence and information on the web.

Social distance   A person who is connected to you not directly, but indirectly through another person, has a greater social distance from you than someone who is directly connected to you.

Social engagement   Effectively connecting with people in an online two-way dialogue.

Social graph   A way of creating a map or a graph showing all of your online connections, their relationship to you and to each other. This will show people who are loosely connected to you via another person and thus have a greater social distance from you.

Social media   A collection of web pages and applications that are designed to allow users to interact with their friends.

Social networking   Interacting with your friends and your friends of friends online.

Social tools   Any website that allows interaction and conversation between its users. Another name for social media.

Strong tie   A close interpersonal relationship with an online connection.

Syndication   Website material that is made available to multiple other sites.

Viral effect   Spreading a marketing message across multiple types media using the network of friends and friends of friends.

Virtual worlds   A computer based simulation of a world or environment where users can interact with each other online to play games and inhabit the environment.

Walled garden   A site which is for its members alone and that doesn't permit interactivity with users from another site.

Weak tie   An occasional connection to someone with whom you wouldn't claim to have more than a casual relationship.

Web 2.0   Web applications and websites that are built to allow interaction, information sharing and uploading of user generated content.

Wiki   An editable web page that can have multiple authors.

1 WHY DO WE WANT A SOCIAL MEDIA STRATEGY?

Implementing a social media strategy in your organisation will dramatically change the way you do business.

If you want to connect with your customers and discover what they think about your brand, social media will help. If you want to change perceptions about your company, or improve your customer service, social media will help. If you want to find out who the influencers and advocates are and get them to broadcast your message on your behalf, then social media will identify the key people in your network whom you should engage with. For you as an individual, if you want to be strategic in your networking goals and you intend to extend your connections by meeting more people, social media will help you reach more people than you ever thought was possible.

With social media in your business, you have a great opportunity to learn more from those around you and discover new information from your extended network. In the right social networks you could discover what you're missing out on in your career, and could create an opening to broaden your perspectives and job prospects. This massive extended virtual network gives you the chance to progress in your professional life using a wider set of connections. You can find a business mentor, advertise your presence or build the relationship to close that deal.

Using social software inside an organisation will also help you achieve an increase in productivity and a reduction in your long term costs.

Companies have spent large sums of money on collaboration software, and yet they don't utilise their investment effectively. There are still multiple islands of data stored in huge storage area networks, which are effectively dead data. Without an effective search mechanism inside a company, without updates, audit notifications and user interaction, this data ages, becomes obsolete and dies. With software providing effective collaboration and interaction securely inside companies, this data has the potential to remain dynamic, engaging and an asset to the company. This social computing environment can then benefit teams, organisations and positively impact the company's customers.

So what does the phenomenal growth in social media interaction mean for your business? With iPod application downloads hitting an astonishing 1 billion in 9 months, what does that mean for Apple's business? What could this mean for your future revenue stream? What potential can you tap into by using this new way of communicating to your advantage?

There have been many articles and discussions about social media and social networking and the potential opportunities they can bring to companies. There are myriad benefits for corporations that choose to leverage this form of communication and use the **conversation** as a digital marketing tool to help them with community engagement or to present the opportunity to increase revenue and market share.

> One of the cardinal rules of social networking is that it's all about giving rather than receiving.

You contribute to the greater sum of knowledge by adding your perspective, know-how, advice, anecdotal stories or links to other sources of knowledge. And there are myriad ways that you can share this information. There are so many tools with odd names that define the term 'social media'. Among them are blogs, moblogging, wikis, tagging, bookmarking, massively multiplayer online role-playing games (MMORPGs), tweets, podcasts, screencasting, vlogs, video, videoblogging, phlogs, video uploads, video sharing, status updates and virtual worlds (I'll explain all of these terms later). Where on earth do you start? Which mechanism is right for your corporate social strategy and which do you need to avoid? What is the process to use for a successful strategy? Where is your plan?

There are several steps to think of in order to achieve success with social networking both inside and outside the organisation.

> These steps are not meant to be used in isolation if a successful strategy is to be followed.

Digital engagement allows us to solve a specific business problem, to connect more effectively with our customers, to listen to their challenges, to help them and to gain advocates who are brand evangelists. Knowing what challenges you want to overcome helps you to set the first part of your strategy in motion, and having a clear plan in place for your business helps you on the first few steps on your journey.

SOCIALLY CONNECTED

I discovered IT quite late in life compared to most of my peers. I'd never considered computing as a career when I was at school, I had gained limited experience with very basic computer programming on a computer science O-level class. I learned binary and I tried to get my head around very basic computing concepts.

I remember the delight I felt on writing my first FOR NEXT loop that actually worked when the program was initiated. I was obviously more of a technician than a scholar. I didn't want to learn about Babbage's engine, I was much keener to learn how the mechanical parts of the computer read the punch tape and converted the tape into characters. I also had other plans for my career. I left school after taking my O levels as I had decided to pursue something completely different and was determined to follow my goal.

I joined the Merchant Navy as a deck cadet on a four-year apprenticeship with Shell Tankers and completely forgot all about computers. Instead I immersed myself in learning how to navigate an oil tanker, load and discharge cargo and maintain the ship's physical condition with gallons of gloss paint and a chipping hammer. In the late 1970s satellite navigation systems were rare, and even if they were installed on board, they were only accurate to about 1 mile. Instead we relied on using logarithmic tables, sextants and the haversine formula to complete our navigation calculations and mark the ship's position by the stars and the sun. I passed my exams, becoming the first female deck officer to sail with Shell Tankers, and I had fulfilled my childhood dream.

I left the sea and joined a container shipping company, working in their office as a containership planner. If the vessel was late in port, due to bad weather or cargo loading delays, then it naturally followed that she would arrive later in every other port on her journey. Cargo space on the vessel was sold by the shipping agents up to 3 months in advance; containers were loaded and delivered to a specific schedule to meet the vessel. It was vital that the shipping agents were well aware of any delays to the vessel's arrival time.

There was a personal computer (PC) on every floor of the shipping company, running Windows 3.11, WordStar and Lotus 123 version 2. It tended to be used to print memos created in the DOS version of WordStar which were occasionally faxed to the ship captains. One day I had an epiphany. I worked out that I could transfer my paper based ships schedule to the spreadsheet in Lotus 123, I could update an entry in one cell of the spreadsheet. Each port in the route could be updated with the new date of either arrival or departure. The spreadsheet would automatically adjust the rest of the schedule for the next 3 months whilst still maintaining the actual historical record of arrival and departure dates. It seems so obvious now, but back then, amongst the team of container planners who had been working using manual methods for years, it was a total revelation.

This simple spreadsheet simplified working across the whole team and made us much more productive.

My love affair with technology and social collaboration began. I realised that I was really good at teaching users about technical – and not so technical – concepts. I loved finding out and explaining how things worked.

I accepted a job as a technical trainer at a Microsoft training provider in London and I suddenly realised that I'd found my niche in technology. I became a Microsoft Certified Professional (MCP) on NT 3.51. I became a Microsoft Certified Trainer (MCT). I then became a Microsoft Certified Systems Engineer (MCSE) with the Internet certification to the acronym (MCSE+I) shortly afterwards.

I then decided to move on to another challenge. I joined Hewlett-Packard as a presales consultant before joining Microsoft as a technical specialist in the Enterprise team.

My skills gained with AS400 systems in the shipping company proved valuable to the presales specialist team. I spent a couple of years talking to enterprise customers about Windows Server before moving to the Evangelism team to talk about technology to the IT Pro audience. The IT Pro team consisted of four evangelists, an architect and a manager – a very small team who had to reach an audience of around 1 million IT professionals in the UK. Our main metrics were to improve audience satisfaction and reach. But apart from the *TechNet* newsletter and the Microsoft website, how would we connect with people we didn't already know?

We started to use social media, specifically blogging, to reach out and talk about what was happening with technology. Back in 2004, YouTube hadn't yet been purchased by Google so we hosted our own 'blogcasts' – short how-to videos and demos of technology with our voiceover, hosted on a server and linked to from our blogs. We used the technical community to record other blogcasts for us and propagate information on their community sites.

> This free sharing of information was mutually beneficial to both the team and the technical community. The resulting videos also benefited users who wanted to learn more about technology.

The community could raise their online profile and demonstrate their technical know-how to their followers, and the team weren't so stretched in resources to produce these videos. I'd discovered the value of using the extended network to benefit both parties.

I became manager of the team in 2005, working on new ways to connect with different audiences in a global market using different types of social media mechanisms and tools. I stayed at Microsoft until 2009 when I left to start out on my own. I could then really focus on the things that connect people.

ONLINE AND FACE TO FACE NETWORKING

I'd been fascinated with social media for a while, but when someone asked me whether social networking was any different from networking physically with people, I realised that there are a lot of similarities in the way I behave online and offline. A lot of the face to face meetings I've had are with people I originally started to connect with online. I've met my virtual connections at a 'tweetup' (a Twitter meetup) or at an online business networking event, and sometimes I've moved forward to meet them in person. Some of these connections will turn into valuable business relationships, others will be tenuous connections or ties to other people. These casual connections communicate infrequently with me online. When I'm at a face to face networking or business event, I collect business cards, some from people who turn out to be valuable connections and some from people I will never hear from again. However, I've been amazed by some fantastic and inspirational people at physical events, and with a little effort to make contact and really connect this has turned up some valuable business and personal contacts for me both online and offline. I've made some great online connections after physical networking events and I stay in touch with these people much more often than I would have done after a traditional business card exchange.

Face to face networking, according to the Harvard Business school, 'is about building a portfolio of relationships that will help you to continue to develop your career'. These relationships will thrive if you know what is going on around you. The same applies to online networking too.

> If you want to progress in business, don't wait to be discovered. Make sure you have a great online profile and a positive brand.

Keeping close tabs on what is going on, being an active contributor, with valid opinions, information and advice, will raise your profile and help you progress in your career.

I network in lots of different ways – face to face, on the phone, via email, text, online and by using social media. This form of online networking keeps me in touch with so many more people than just email or phone does. I get a huge buzz from connecting people who can help each other out. It gives me a great satisfaction to actually make that connection. So it's not all about my work.

Your world of friends and family, colleagues and business connections is defined by the people you are connected to. Some of your friends know each other; some of your friends are isolated in your social circle. Some of your connections will be farther out in distance from your close family. Some will be people in your address book whom you hardly ever see, others will be connected to you in some way on a daily basis. You can map your connections in the form of a graph. This is your 'social graph', with your more distant connections mapping to the outskirts of the graph. This 'social distance' defines the limits of your graph. But it can provide the gateway to join you to other graphs.

There are tools that leverage the connections in your own social graph and online sites that make it really easy to connect with your friends and the friends of your friends. These online tools make it simple to meet and connect with people in similar situations who can then make more people aware of you and your capabilities. You can make connections across the board with senior colleagues, competitors, and local business people – even with politicians perhaps? It is possible. You want

5

to meet people who can help you – but where can you find them? There are online connections with your colleagues and IT peers, your friends and family and your friends' friends. There are professional associations and networks, vendors and consultants who could be connected to you. It really does seem like social networking has become an amazing business enabler.

I've been immersed in collaborative technology for over 15 years and it has changed my perspective about the world around me. I've used social networking tools from time to time since I started in IT, and it was only when I started thinking about which social media mechanisms I use inside and outside my workplace, especially when I travel, that I realised just how much it was a key part of my life.

I've been a lurker, a listener, a broadcaster, a conversationalist and an influencer. I've asked for help in forums, talked to strangers using chat software and created videos to help people out. I've shared interesting and not so interesting facts, initially by email to my friends, latterly through my blog, and now on Twitter, Facebook, LinkedIn, YouTube and SlideShare. I've used several different types of tools to syndicate my news and information across other sites so that contacts in different realms can keep in touch. I have a fairly consistent online brand, and searches for eileenb, my online brand profile name, get the searcher to all of the sites I intend it to. But it's my own social behaviour that makes me curious.

Why do I continue this level of interaction with my virtual friends and connections, lots of whom I've never met? What drives this altruistic behaviour, this desire of mine to help others? Is this a desire to connect or communicate, inform or engage? Do I want to convert others to my way of thinking by regularly interacting with my circle of friends, colleagues and connections? Or do I want to try and persuade my friends in my immediate network to tell their friends who are outside my directly connected network about the latest and greatest in technology? What drives my behaviour?

To find out why I do this, I began to take a closer look at the mechanisms behind it. I wanted to find out why it has become such a key part of the digital marketing, community and advertising strategy. I wanted to understand why this mechanism effectively connects you with your customers, amplifies your message and engages your audience. I wanted to know how this network – the 'word of mouth network', or the '**world** of mouth network' – has become such a powerful tool to use in business in the 21st century.

2   THE NEW WAY OF COMMUNICATING

Social media is not something that will burst like the South Sea bubble or the dotcom bubble. This is not something that will pass you or your company by. Social computing has far reaching effects that will permeate every business, reaching all job roles. It is worldwide and pervasive. So what are you doing about it?

Everyone seems to be talking about push–pull marketing, with tools and sites offering get-rich-quick schemes and easy ways to increase your followers. Why has there been so much exposure for this new way of communication? To consider this, we need to look at the key drivers for us to connect with others online.

We need to connect – with another entity across the town, the country, the world. Our need to interact virtually with each other has driven a massive explosion of Web 2.0 applications, designed to help you connect, communicate, snoop and stalk. But it is becoming harder to function effectively in today's technology-obsessed world without effort or seeming to become an Internet geek. The Web 2.0 world can be looked at from many different angles. You can watch the effect that Web 2.0 has had on ordinary consumers and the way they now interact with the web.

> Watching how social networks grow across different environments has resulted in a fundamental change in society, technology and business practices.

We begin by looking at how people interact in social groups, both face to face and online, looking at how Generation Y behave on social networking sites and how their behaviour differs from that of the baby boomers. We look at how the conversation between consumers and companies has changed over time into a two-way dialogue and how some companies have benefited from this effect. We then look back to when online social conversation began and how the early bulletin boards, chat rooms and multi-user dungeons have evolved into forums, instant messaging and MMORPGs. We also look at the evolution of the Internet for consumers, the rise of Internet service providers and proprietary forum software such as CompuServe and AOL. We see how walled gardens prevented cross-network interaction and how browsers worked to get around this issue. We then look at how the concept of Web 2.0 changed the way that users interacted with websites and companies, and how social networks grew to take advantage of this interaction. Finally, we discuss the influencers inside the organisation and explain how these influencers connect, network and propagate information across business groups. We see how adding extra information to the conversation encourages dialogue to flow more readily and effectively builds your network.

IS THIS THE NEW FAD FOR THE 21ST CENTURY?

People like to live in groups – family groups, work groups, hobby groups, sport groups. Since the dawn of time we have connected with each other to grow food, eat, form families, procreate, declare our religious allegiance and fight wars. So, with the advent of PCs and the Internet, what has changed? Nothing, as it turns out. We connect to others to form groups. But nowadays there are digital groups as well as groups for our usual day to day human to human interaction.

> People on the Internet tend to interact with each other in social, trusting and communal ways, and this is what makes the explosion of digital interactivity and interconnectedness so powerful.

From the early days of online activity, before CompuServe, people have interacted with each other electronically. I remember how CompuServe issued a series of numbers to represent user names, and I struggled to connect my 300 baud modem to the Internet by dialling the CompuServe access number on my phone and placing the handset into the soft rubber cradle on the modem hardware device. In the early 1990s, the advent of forums, newsgroups and Internet Relay Chat led to an explosion in interaction with the Web. With Web 2.0 we have been trying to connect digitally in much the same way. There are gardening forums, recipes, dating sites, pornography, religious sites and virtual gaming worlds. We are striving to connect in the same social groups and achieve the same personal goals – but now we want to do it online.

Social networking, and thereby social media, lies at the heart of these connections – and by creating, maintaining and cultivating valuable interactions with the connections in your local and remote hubs, your networks can grow and thrive.

> Companies that have an effective social engagement strategy in place, with a manageable timescale and structured implementation plan, can find their customers, identify who the movers and shakers are, and connect effectively with them.

They can watch who is active in the markets they want to go into, check the sentiments of their audiences' messages and listen for their challenges. Relationships can be built carefully on a one to one basis. Detractors can be turned into advocates, who can be encouraged with an appropriate programme to become key enthusiasts broadcasting and amplifying your message on your behalf.

So is the great conversation just the new buzzword of the new millennium? Or is it actually the biggest shift in human behaviour since the industrial revolution? For this we need to look at the new 'generations'. Baby boomers include people who were born after the Second World War between 1945 and about 1962. Generation X includes people who were born from 1963 to approximately 1979. Generation Y, or the Millennial Generation, includes those born from 1980 to 2000. Generation Z are those who have been born in the 21st century. The Generation Y population now, in 2010, outnumbers the baby boomer population, and 96% of the Generation Y crowd have joined some sort of social network for interaction. These social networks are changing the way we communicate in a fundamental way. We no longer search for news – the news now finds us. Soon we will no longer search for products or services – these products and services will find us via social media.

They key thing here is not that we communicate digitally, rather the particular ways we do so.

You can't pick the 'winning' medium and ignore what your friends and colleagues are using.

Different mechanisms of communicating using conversational tools may bubble up to the top in popularity for a time, but the fundamental concepts behind how we use these products to communicate are the same throughout each network. These engagement applications are here to stay. Of course, the actual applications themselves will morph into something else, applications for mobile phones will come to prominence, and new technologies that use social media to connect will appear. Old and poorly designed applications will fade into obscurity. We're living in the age of the perpetual beta, and we need to learn to evolve with these technologies and adapt to take advantage of this new way of working. Our challenge is to learn how to adapt to the new way of working in a dynamic and rapidly changing world and work out how social media actually works for us as an individual, colleague, parent and friend.

This fundamental shift in the way we communicate has the ability to transcend boundaries. Barack Obama conducted his presidential election campaign on Twitter and YouTube. He successfully encouraged a significant number of Americans to vote for him, who would not normally have bothered to follow the campaign or vote. He continued this effective online presence with a conference in March 2009 answering questions using a voting style popular on the information channel Digg. He even appears to have a LinkedIn profile. On a more personal level, the video of Susan Boyle, an ordinary contestant on a UK talent show with an extraordinary voice, has been viewed over 120 million times on YouTube, catapulting her into the limelight and millionaire status within 6 months of her first appearance.

For corporate users, embracing this change can be beneficial in more ways than one. A common criticism from consumers is that companies don't listen to them, don't care about the people who buy their goods. Customers feel that once the

9

goods or services have been purchased, the customer care programmes are poor or non-existent. Companies are often vilified for bringing out 'new and improved' products after poor market research and with little consideration for the customer. They are accused of launching new products that are not ready for the market, that don't fit customer requirements, or fail customers' expectations. On the other hand, there are some companies whose fan base is the envy of the market. Think of the passion that Apple invokes across the technology sector, with new products announced to a joyful fan base and queues of potential purchasers camped out outside the Apple store, desperate to be one of the first to own one of the shiny new gadgets. Think of the hoards of Harley-Davidson aficionados, some of whom are happy to have the brand as a tattoo on their bodies – a permanent reminder of their loyalty. Think of the consumers who will only drink Starbucks coffee and eschew all other brands. Think of the image of Rolls Royce, of Perrier, of Gucci and Coca-Cola.

But what if your company doesn't have this level of loyalty, dedication and support from your customers? Ideally you want to grow your market share, win customers' loyalty perhaps from a competitor and improve perception of your company in the marketplace.

> Consider incorporating push–pull conversations into your traditional strategy as a new mechanism for reaching your audience.

You may have considered extending your traditional marketing approach and current online marketing strategy and you may have plans to embrace the world of Web 2.0. The prospect of interacting with your customers, the people who actually buy your products and services, can give you the opportunity to extend your reach into new, global markets, and connect more closely with your online audience.

WHY DO YOU NEED SOCIAL CONNECTIONS?

In his book, *The Tipping Point*,[1] Malcolm Gladwell describes three types of people – connectors, mavens and salesmen:

> Connectors are the people who 'link us up with the world, people with a special gift for bringing the world together. They are "a handful" of people with an extraordinary knack for making friends and acquaintances'. These individuals typically have social networks of over one hundred people. Connectors gain success in 'their ability to span many different worlds as a function of something intrinsic to their personality, some combination of curiosity, self-confidence, sociability, and energy.'
>
> Mavens are 'information specialists', or 'people we rely upon to connect us with new information.' They accumulate knowledge, especially about the marketplace,

and know how to share it with others. 'A Maven is someone who wants to solve other people's problems, generally by solving his own. Mavens start "word-of-mouth epidemics" due to their knowledge, social skills, and ability to communicate, they are information brokers, sharing and trading what they know'.

Salesmen are 'persuaders', charismatic people with powerful negotiation skills. They tend to have an indefinable trait that goes beyond what they say, which makes others want to agree with them.

Each of these categories of people can potentially become your 'first tier' influencers. These are the people that are **directly** connected to you in some way. They follow news about your brand. They discuss your brand with their connections. They want to have a closer dialogue with you. They are all influencers in their own right and, with their own specific skills, can reach out beyond your immediate network to influence others. Your tier 1 influencers can connect to your tier 2 influencers, who can also help to spread the word about your brand.

If you can find people in your immediate network who have these qualities you can start to engage in dialogue with them, cultivate them and give them information.

If you can find some information that is not generally available externally it will be very well received. Mavens will relish these bits of 'special' information – they will broker the information to the connectors and salesmen in their networks, and the message gets out. Each type of information gatherer will connect in some way to the next tier of influencers which may be further away from you in social distance, but closer to others in their own networks.

TIER 1 INFLUENCERS

- Tier 1 influencers typically hang out on user forums, they help out in community sites and they often have the answers the community needs.

- They respond to questions posed on the forum, or, if they are connector types, they will know someone in their network who does have the answer if they don't actually know it themselves.

- They may run user groups or attend them.

- They are forum moderators.

- They run user Q&A portals and participate in chat rooms.

- They are often quick to respond to a question posted on Twitter or Facebook.

- They are significant in your 'fan-out' evangelism efforts.

Fan-out messaging works like this. I tell two people, who each tell two people, who each tell two people, who each tell two people. My original message has fanned out and has reached 30 new potential customers – or, more importantly, potential influencers for my brand. These influencers and their connections are vital in getting your message out on your behalf. They retweet your interesting news on Twitter, they link to your blog from their own blog and they share useful links on Facebook. This network rebroadcasts and amplifies your message for you.

Tier 1 influencers are often early adopters. They buy the latest gadget, phone and eBook reader. They beta-test new releases of software and often have the latest and greatest laptop. They demonstrate their new hardware to anyone who will watch. They download the latest Twitter client and tweet endlessly about it. I remember the hype about the first iPhone. When it was released in the US in June 2007, hundreds of keen consumers queued for up to 12 hours outside the Apple store to be among the first to own it. They broadcast this to their friends through blogs, Facebook and Twitter. These influencers created a buzz about the device which ensured that a huge amount of people got to hear about it through the reports in the newswires. Now, the iPhone is the most popular mobile device in the US.[2] Apple has the ability to cause ripples around the online world with its new products, as the rumours about the alleged theft of their prototype 4G iPhone showed in April 2010.

Large companies have structured rewards and incentives programmes for influencers who are not usually motivated by financial incentives, but who thrive on knowledge gathering, community and recognition. IBM maintains an Influencer programme for its consultants and integrators, and another for its Partner Resellers. Microsoft has its Most Valuable Professionals programme and Intel has an innovative Intel Insiders programme. This new programme gained an award for innovation in new media in its second year of operation from the Society for New Communications Research in December 2009. Ferrari has a well established community of fans, most of whom have never owned a Ferrari but who continue to give the brand prominence throughout the world. For other examples of brand loyalists, enthusiasts and advocates, you only need to think of Nike, Burberry, Harley-Davidson, Marmite and Calvin Klein.

> If you get your key influencers right then your tier 1 and your tier 2 influencers will do the job of getting your message out for you.

If you maintain a close relationship with your tier 1 influencers they will reward you by broadcasting your message for you. Software beta testers willingly try out incomplete software products for the chance to further their knowledge and appear more technically advanced than their peers. Airlines get loyalty from their travellers with Air Miles programmes and frequent flyer clubs, and supermarkets offer incentives through their loyalty and rewards cards. Coffee shops have simple loyalty cards offering free cake or coffee after a certain number of purchases. Even my local car wash at the back of the DIY store offers to give me my seventh car wash free. Of course I take full advantage of this!

If you invest time in maintaining the relationship with your tier 1 influencers, you will find you have a great circle of loyal advocates to spread the word about your brand. These influencers will greatly increase the amount of coverage when they talk about your product or gizmo, so it's worthwhile talking about it. If you don't think you have the time to invest in talking about your product across your channels, then spending 30 minutes a day promoting your message can still be of benefit if it is done outside your immediate circle of connections.

THE NEW WAY OF MARKETING TO YOUR CUSTOMERS

As social media becomes more prevalent in every part of our lives then so do questions about future trends in technology. What will be the next big thing to catch our attention? Where is social media going and how will it evolve? How will our behaviour change to adapt to this new way of communicating? How will our working patterns change? Will we have to do more with less, or will we become completely overwhelmed with the additional tasks we will have to perform in this Web 2.0 world?

We're experiencing a huge shift in our marketing too. The new way of working involves interaction and conversation, engagement and advocacy. Our approach has got to change to incorporate this. Traditional marketing methods now have to include a digital marketing component as part of the overall strategy. Now the old, push ways of marketing have to evolve and incorporate two-way dialogue which encourages conversation with the new thought leaders. And who are these new thought leaders? Well, they are everyone with access to the Internet and a set of friends, followers and connections.

> Our customers, our consumers have become the new marketers who drive the conversation about our brands.

They are the new thought leaders and they will shape the way that the company operates. Ensuring longevity of followers in a marketing campaign will also become a priority. During a campaign there will be much activity and therefore awareness, but as activity decreases after the campaign so awareness declines and follower churn sets in.

> The need to continue the conversation is becoming more and more relevant.

Regular engagement and interaction add significant value to the conversation and awareness of the brand. Campaigns should be created with repeat engagement in mind to encourage regular interaction and repeat visits.

Marketing departments will have to switch from their current outbound marketing campaigns and listen to the inbound voices. Traditional advertising behaviours will change from broadcasting **at** the consumer to listening **to** them.

The voice of the consumer will become the only voice to listen to, and companies will need to take advantage of their new listening skills. Subject matter experts will have a much louder influence over companies, as their messages will be amplified by the community. They will become the new influencers, advocates, critics and detractors. Companies will **have** to listen to this new voice.

Intelligent companies will be aware of the groundswell of conversation. They will work with their customers and advocates.

Intelligent companies will cultivate strong positive relationships by creating and maintaining their influencer connections, and they will reward their customers.

They will do this through a series of rewards programmes and they will showcase these advocates as an extension of the company itself.

Marketers will adopt the new mechanism of communications, and more and more marketing efforts will focus on a dialogue with customers instead of a one-way outbound broadcast in a marketing campaign.

This will result in consumer brand value and perception changes as the two-way dialogue becomes a structured conversation.

Marketing success will no longer be measured in terms of numbers reached, as sentiment and the **two-way conversation** will be considered important.

Social media sites already offer great opportunities to engage with and influence customers in ways that are different from traditional marketing approaches.

This engagement with sentiment that can be captured almost in real time can offer a baseline for customer perception and identify key influencers.

Many social campaigns, however, currently have mixed results due to the lack of time investment and social presence.

The needs of different audiences should be also taken into account when planning campaigns. Groups of consumers, prosumers (professionals who use technology to do their job), technologists, influencers and hobbyists all have different requirements from a campaign and these behaviours should be taken into account when targets are set.

SUMMARY

- Social media is the new way of communicating online. It will not go away, so you need to adapt your working practices to take advantage of the new conversation.

- Having an effective social media plan in place helps you to effectively connect with your customers.

- Consider implementing push–pull conversations into your strategy.

- There are three types of communicators: connectors, mavens and salesmen. These are your influencers.

- Consider creating an incentives plan for your influencers.

- Intelligent companies will cultivate strong relationships with their influencers and enjoy a shift in perceptions of the company.

- Companies need to invest time and effort in their social media planning.

3 YOUR SOCIAL MEDIA SUCCESS PLAN

There are fundamental tenets to the way to behave in the new world of conversation, and having a good implementation plan in place is essential. There are things you can put in place so you can be successful in social media, and there are behaviours you can adopt so that people will communicate with you.

HOW TO BE SUCCESSFUL WITH SOCIAL MEDIA

- Know where your audience is.
- Don't fish in stagnant water – go where the fresh water flows. Choose dynamic sites with plenty of interaction.
- Give more than you receive. Contribute and interact to engage in dialogue.
- Become valuable to your readers.
- Be sociable.
- Discover who your online advocates are.
- Build a relationship with your influencers inside organisations.
- Understand your social graph, your key connectors and their social distance from other key connectors.
- Define metrics for success. Don't evaluate the return on your investment by using traditional numerical metrics, but by softer metrics such as comments, sentiment and trends.

Most sales and marketing organisations want some form of return from their actions. They want to be able to see a measurable result. They pay for advertising and want an increase in sales. They hold sales activities and want to have sales. They change their website, run a campaign and want a measurable increase in visitors to the site. Unfortunately social media doesn't work on such a transactional basis. It is fluid and dynamic, it is people-centric and disorganised. The social media revolution is powered by people and that's why it can never be transactional.

Many have jumped onto the social networking scene and not been successful. They have registered with every social media site that they have come across and they have found themselves overwhelmed. They wonder how they are going to manage to keep up with all of the information flowing at them and do their job too. Without a good plan in place it is really difficult to carry out their activities in a consistent way to connect with their audience. There are only so many hours in a day for you to keep up with this onslaught of information and stay sane, so here are some recommendations to help you be productive – not destructive.

KEEPING IT UNDER CONTROL

- Be consistent. Try to maintain a regular pattern in your communications on the web. Burst blogging (or tweeting) techniques are annoying to your audience and add extra load to your day. If you have a relatively easy day, then post-date some of your blog posts so that your readers get a regular update. Aim to tweet regularly too and maintain the connection with your audience.

- Don't get overwhelmed. There are so many different social networking sites out there that it's so easy to become flooded with information. If you spend all day on Twitter, or try to keep up with all of the status updates and changes on Facebook, you won't have any time at all for the rest of the things you need to do. You need to learn to cut out all the unnecessary messages. There are some users who seem to have no life beyond their online presence, and other users who smack of desperation. Try to maintain a happy balance, filter out those messages you don't want to see, and be ruthless with the unfollow button. Do you really need all those friends? Are they valuable connections for your business or automated bots looking for keywords or followers?

- Syndication – is it really necessary? You may have accounts on multiple networking sites and update each of them regularly with the same information. However, there are issues with this approach. If you maintain multiple personas on different sites, and share different kinds of information with different social groups, they may not appreciate business related updates on their personal network with you. Additionally, there might be some friends who follow you on many of your social networking sites and who may not appreciate the same information on each of their sites.

- Don't dismiss forums. People come to forums for advice. Often they are unaware that there are other resources available. If you contribute to forums, make sure you cross-reference your information to your blog. It drives traffic to your blog, and connects up the different resources. You can also point people who ask questions on forums to other social networking sites to help them.

- Be generous. If you have knowledge – share it! There are many, many people out there who are thirsty for knowledge. Share it appropriately. Be professional and courteous. Remember that not everyone has the same level of knowledge as you have, so don't flame them unnecessarily.

- Don't expect instant results. Your followers will visit your blog or follow you on Twitter, Facebook or LinkedIn and come back if they like your content. Don't expect to get thousands and thousands of readers in a day. Expect to build up gradually. Ignore all of those Twitter followers that promise a thousand followers a day. They are automated bots of little value to you. You want to have connections to real human beings.

- Deal appropriately with undesirables. If someone wants to connect with you and you don't want them to, don't feel guilty about denying the connection or blocking the follow on Twitter. Generally the person is not notified that you have rejected the connection, and if you have blocked them, they will not be able to contact you further. Don't encourage abuse by accepting connections you do not want. It's time wasting and demoralising.

- Get connected. Like syndication, your blog has your personality stamped onto it. So advertise it. People **want** to connect with you. Place a link to your blog on every online profile you have. You will drive traffic to your blog. If you have a Twitter account, refer to your Twitter handle wherever possible on online sites.

- Sell if you can, but don't sell directly. If you are selling something, don't be afraid to talk about it, evangelise it, discuss it – but don't allow your desire to sell overwhelm your voice. The constant sell will soon become wearing to your readers who will dismiss you as spam.

- Interact. Social Networking is **not** one-way communication. It's the interactions between the participants that make social networking – social. Take advantage of the connections you make to forge new customer relationships and enlarge your virtual network. People with a common interest will follow you, so will really appreciate the personal connection from you.

Many companies don't ask themselves why they are going to implement a social media plan. Often they feel that they need to introduce some sort of activity and use social media as a broadcast channel only. Having an effective conversational plan in place will make you more successful than having a one-way broadcast mechanism. Incorporating metrics will help you with your conversations with key stakeholders. Here are some things to think about and questions to ask.

THINGS TO CONSIDER IN YOUR SOCIAL MEDIA STRATEGY

- Why do you want to incorporate social media into your business? Who do you want to connect with? What results do you want to achieve? How will you measure success?

- Do you want to use specific individuals in your organisation for outbound communication with your external community, or do you intend to include everyone within the company to help you deliver your message?

- Do you know what platform you intend to use to broadcast your efforts? Do you want to focus your efforts on free networking services such as Twitter, Blogger, Facebook, Wordpress and YouTube?

- Do you want to expose your existing collaboration platform like Lotus Notes or Microsoft SharePoint through the firewall for better customisation of the interface and control?

- Do you want to tie your new online conversational strategy back to your company initiatives? There is significant business value to be gained by engaging with your audience using social media, but you need to make sure you focus on your objectives.

- Have you defined your desired results and timescale to achieve your goals? Have you detailed which metrics you want to achieve, and the tools you need to use to measure your success? These tools are important when you tie your achievements back to your strategy.

- Do you have the key points of your strategy in a crystal clear format which can be explained simply to the decision makers at board level?

- Before you launch your plan, have you listened to the conversation before starting to speak yourself? Your audience may not want to hear what you're telling them. By listening, responding and then joining into the conversation, you'll be well on the way to measurable success.

MEASUREMENTS AND METRICS

When you've decided on the tools you're going to use, make sure that you execute your strategy with a defined goal and a defined timescale, say 6 months or a year. Make this implementation plan realistic and start to introduce each tool gradually. As an example, you could devise a plan that executes for a year and consists of the following steps:

SOCIAL MEDIA ONE-YEAR PLAN

- Engage with multiple blogs, forums and wikis covering issues relating to your product or brand. Comment regularly. Start to create a dialogue.

- Create a blog. Try to blog regularly about interesting and useful topics that your readers would be interested in. Include your blog URL on your email auto-signature and on your website. Aim for 100 blog posts per year with an average of 300–400 views per post. Measure comments on your blog, and aim to comment on other blogs at least once per day. This leads viewers of other blogs back to your blog.

- Create a Technorati account and aim to increase your Technorati influence by tagging your posts so that they are easily discovered.

- Create a Twitter account. Include your blog URL on your Twitter profile; include your website URL on your blog. Talk about your Twitter stream on your blog; perhaps embed tweets from Twitter on your blog. Plan to tweet about twice a day and respond to other Twitter comments. Aim to increase your following

> with valuable users who are real people whom you can engage with and not automated bots.
>
> - Create a Facebook page that refers to your blog and your Twitter stream URLs. Start conversations and encourage customers to interact and give feedback to your Facebook page from both Twitter and your blog.
>
> - Start a YouTube channel which points to your blog and Twitter. Upload videos regularly. Encourage dialogue and comments. Answer comments. Refer to your YouTube channel from Facebook, Twitter and your blog.
>
> - Start a channel on UStream (or a similar video streaming service) with embedded Twitter stream for live interaction from your customers. Advertise it on each of your other social media channels and advertise all of your other communications channels on UStream.
>
> - Develop a series of webcasts to help customers with any areas they're struggling with on your product or brand. Publish them on channels such as YouTube, Vimeo, MSN Video and Videojug.

Whatever mechanism you use to measure success, you need to have a set of measures and metrics before you start to execute your strategy. Start with a realistic baseline of your online presence and conversations about you. Set a reasonable timescale for metric measurements to be taken. Create your digital and social media policy, making sure it concurs with employee policy. Train your staff in the use of the tools you intend to use, make sure that they are fully aware of your social media corporate guidelines and policy and ask them to use your chosen channels to communicate. After a reasonable period of time measure your success, tracking any feedback and progress you've made through each of these channels. If you haven't defined your baseline metrics, then you will find it very difficult to measure your return on investment (ROI) and your success with your efforts. Your measures of success could be related to the increase in the number of people who are engaging with you and your brand. You could also benefit from an improvement in your conversations with your customers and advocates due to your closer connection to your customers.

It's a great idea to have a social media corporate policy and a strategy about the types of tools you will use to reach your customers. It's also commendable if your work environment and corporate values encourage your teams to use social software to reach your customers. However, if you have no definable way of measuring the impact that your outreach efforts actually have on your intended audience, your implementation plan will be hard to justify to the budget owners in the company.

As with all of your other business objectives, you need to have a way of effectively gathering data from your customers and measuring your key performance indicators. Unfortunately, as there are many tools used to broadcast your message across all of the social channels, then there isn't one particular metrics tool you can use to track your success. But what sorts of metrics do you want for the result you need to achieve? Do your metrics depend on the number of connections you have on Facebook or LinkedIn? Do you want to track the number of fans on your

Facebook group page or the number of members in your LinkedIn Group? Do you want to measure the number of followers you have on Twitter? Do you count numbers? Or do you want to measure interaction, influence, sentiment, mood or revenue? Whatever your goal happens to be, you need to be able to measure these metrics in a structured way.

Defining your targets

There are many tools, both free and commercial, that you can use to track trends and metrics for your campaign. Facebook's Friend Wheel application measures who is in your social graph and how well connected your tier 1 connections are in Facebook. There are other social graph applications and there are lots of Twitter tools like Twitter Grader and TweetStats that show how highly valued your profile is or whether your topic is trending right now on Twitter. Tracking your chosen metrics means that you will need to watch your online channels regularly. Over time you can get a month on month increase in readers, engagement or links clicked and record any comments that have been written. You can then compare the reach you achieve on these channels with the reach you achieve on your paid media channels which will give you an idea of their ongoing value to you.

NUMBERS OR INTERACTION?

- Do you want to track the increase in the number of people reading your company blog?
- Do you want your blog readers to increase their interaction with you by commenting on your blog?
- Do you want your users to fill in a satisfaction survey twice a year so you can see how your customers perceive your company or your brand?
- Do you want to measure change in perception of your company?
- Do you want increase awareness of your brand or sub-brand?
- Do you want to measure increased interaction of users who visit your website, either by measuring their comments on articles you write, page visits, unique users, or responses to online campaigns?

These metrics, such as page views per visitor, unique visitors and time spent on each page, can easily be analysed by an analytics tool such as StatCounter or Google Analytics. But in order to effectively measure interaction and response to your social media efforts you need to think about using some of the metrics to create your baseline.

SOCIAL MEDIA METRICS

Blogging

Number of subscribers (using Feedburner or similar)
Number of web views

Numbers of RSS hits
Number of comments
Number of trackbacks
Number of reposts
Technorati authority
Volume of conversation

User Forums:

Number of new subscribers
Number of new members
Number of new threads
Number of regular posters per month
Number of posts per day
Number of page views
Number of returning unique users
Number of registered users
Response rate
Top 10 ranked questions
Top 10 thread respondents

Twitter:

Number of followers
Number of conversations to @
Number of retweets
Number of URL click-throughs (using a metrics tracker such as bit.ly)
Range of Influence – your people who follow your followers (you can use a software script to automate the process)

Virtual World

Number of visitors
Number of incoming links to a website
Average time on site

Facebook

Number of page fans (people who like the page)
Number of topic discussions
Number of comments / likes

YouTube

Number of views
Number of channel subscribers
Number of comments
Volume of conversation

Photo sharing sites

Number of comments
Number of views
Ranking

Measuring any one of these metrics can be done within your overall strategy and they can help you to measure your ROI. Metrics can also gauge whether you're being successful in your efforts to execute or whether you're failing. This will give you simple figures to show to the board. Your choice of tools depends very much on your marketing strategy and desired outcomes. Here are some of the popular tools used for analysis and metrics:

- BlogPulse
- Brandwatch
- How Sociable
- Google Insights
- GoogleNews
- Market Sentinel
- Nielsen Buzzmetrics
- Omniture
- Onalytica
- Radian6
- Technorati
- Techrigy
- Trendistic
- Twitcalc
- Twitter Trends
- Visible technologies

This all seems like a really simple way to capture your success with social media, but I must sound a note of warning. Beware of depending on one particular product alone for your metrics, and bear in mind that the social media landscape changes frequently. If you're building an application that can be used on networking sites, be wary of nailing your colours to the mast of another social media tool. The site you built your application for might switch allegiance and start to compete with you for business or mindshare.

The music recommendation service iLike, which provides a music application for Facebook, is heavily dependent on its provider.[3] About 80% of iLike's revenue comes from Facebook. iLike has built its entire business on Facebook, and the company was valued at $20 million when MySpace made an offer to buy it. iLike is very dependent on advertising for business and as it has gathered 50 million registered users from Facebook. The issue here is if you have an application that is heavily dependent on a social site's application programming interface, then you are entirely at the mercy of the social site, which may change its terms of use with little or no notice. If iLike were purchased by MySpace, the rival to Facebook, then it could be very difficult for iLike if Facebook decided to withdraw support for the service, and this is also true for several other applications that are heavily dependent on their hosting sites. Changing the terms or the technology could paralyse the relationship.

So don't bank on using one developer platform exclusively for your business opportunity. If the site decides to pull the plug on you, where else could you go?

WHAT IS RIGHT FOR YOUR ORGANISATION?

There are so many different options and channels you can consider implementing, that it can be difficult to make a choice. I've created a simple flow chart (Figure 3.1) to show you your options when you're deciding which channels you could use for your business. Primarily, you need to decide what you want to achieve by using social media tools. Do you want to use the channel for the community or do you want to demonstrate your credibility in the industry? For simplicity, the chart only shows Facebook, Twitter, blogging, LinkedIn and YouTube.

Figure 3.1 Social media tools flowchart

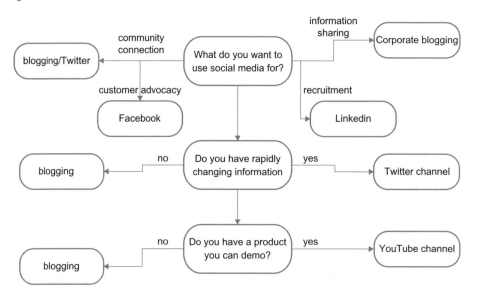

Every company has different outreach requirements and you will use the tools in a different way to achieve a different set of results. All tools can be used for all types of connections to your audience; it's how you use the tools that will make the difference to the way that your customers and partners respond.

Careful consideration of your strategy will also make a big difference to your approach and will help you implement an effective plan. This plan will be closely tied to your corporate objectives with measurable goals and the correct level of investment for the project. Then you will be able to measure your success.

The tools that you use to engage with your customers will be different depending whether your focus is business to business (B2B) or business to consumer (B2C) or you run different campaigns. In Figure 3.2 I've grouped the more popular tools based on their value to the customer in B2B and B2C settings and the impact on your customers if you use them.

Figure 3.2 Tools, their value and impact to the customer

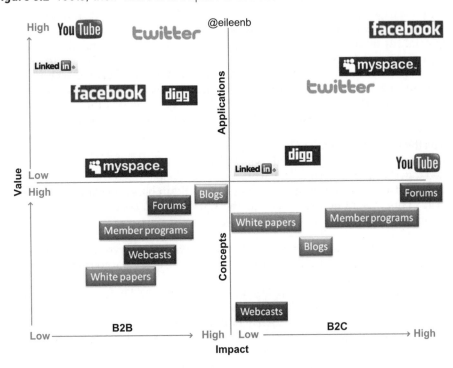

SOCIAL MEDIA IS NOT THE NEW WAY OF COMMUNICATING

Social media is here, and it's here to stay. Our challenge is to take advantage of this and grow both in our home and work lives.

Communicating using these types of tools is not a new concept. It is, however, the buzzword of the moment. There's a plethora of pretty-looking, interactive, engaging applications and hundreds of rival social interaction sites that you can use to communicate and share information with your network of friends and acquaintances.

> We are, and have always been, social animals who live and work together in groups, and it follows that media has been used for social reasons ever since we lived in caves.

What else are cave paintings for if not to show your fellow cave dwellers just how to handle a buffalo? With the advent of digital communications, it was inevitable that we would find ways to connect with each other online.

From the early days of email, people have been forwarding messages to each other, but the bulletin board changed the way that people interacted. Some of the first applications were built to accommodate communication and sharing. For several decades we have been party to one of the biggest cultural shifts since the industrial revolution and have watched the development of a whole host of types of digital interaction. The range extends beyond Facebook and Twitter to more esoteric offerings such as multi-user dungeons from where World of Warcraft and Second Life can trace their origins. Multi-object-oriented applications are used for text based adventure games and education facilities while instant messaging, chat rooms and bulletin boards are more familiar in the mainstream.

The birth of the bulletin board

One of the earliest bulletin boards was Arpanet, where the first terminals were linked together in California in November 1969. People liked the idea of communicating with each other online. One popular bulletin board in California was the WELL.[4] This was launched in 1985 as the Whole Earth 'Lectronic Link and is still running today.

The US was well ahead of the rest of the world when it came to word of mouth networking, bulletin board and forum software. The early pornographic site, Rusty-N-Edie, had some 124 computers and nearly 6,000 subscribers by 1993. Any subscriber living outside the US had to dial in to the US numbers, paying for an international telephone call (Figure 3.3). The site contained 105,000–110,000 files available for downloading, nearly half of which were graphic image files (GIFs). GIFs from Rusty-N-Edie's bulletin board could be downloaded by the customer to his or her home computer, and could be viewed only with specialised software. Some of these 'adult' photos were the subject of a court case between Rusty-N-Edie and Playboy magazine.[5]

Bulletin boards still exist today. A quick search on the web brought me to Monochrome, and there are several websites devoted to bulletin board archives. These simple interactive 'green screen' technologies allowing real-time interaction between users and message passing are considered to be the foundation upon which social media evolved.

Building walled gardens

Unsurprisingly users wanted to have a new and more engaging way of interacting. CompuServe and AOL provided walled gardens for users.

Figure 3.3 Rusty-N-Edie's bulletin board

```
Éííí ííí ííí ííí ííí ííí ííí ííí ííí ííí ííí ííí ííí ííí ííí ííí ííí ííí ííí ííí ííí ííí ííí íí ííí»
  ọ              This program is brought to you with the blessings        ọ
  ọ                     of Rusty n Edie's BBS and its Users.              ọ
  ọ                                                                       ọ
  ọ         We have the largest collection of Public Domain Software      ọ
  ọ              and the largest collection of Adult GIFS & Programs      ọ
  ọ                                                                       ọ
  ọ            OVER 12 GIGS!!!                        112 LINES!!!        ọ
  ọ                                                                       ọ
  ọ                     Call 1 216-726-2620                               ọ
  ọ                        300 / 1200 / 2400                              ọ
  ọ                              or                                       ọ
  ọ                     Call 1 216-726-3589                               ọ
  ọ            U.S. Robotics Dual Standard 14.4kV32 Compatible           ọ
  ọ                              or                                       ọ
  ọ                     Call 1 216-726-3619                               ọ
  ọ                Hayes V-Series V42 9600 / 19200                        ọ
  ọ                              or                                       ọ
  ọ                     Call 1 216-726-3620                               ọ
  ọ                CompuCom SpeedModem 9600 / 19200                       ọ
  ọ                                                                       ọ
  ọ                Accessible Via Connect-USA Node RNEBBS                 ọ
  ọ                Accessible Via Starlink Node: 4909                     ọ
  ọ                                                                       ọ
  ọ            WE ARE THE FRIENDLIEST BBS IN THE WORLD!                   ọ
Èííí ííí ííí ííí ííí ííí ííí ííí ííí ííí ííí ííí ííí ííí ííí ííí ííí ííí ííí ííí ííí ííí ííí íí ííí¼
```

> Walled gardens are sites where members of that site can chat to other members of that site.

Walled gardens, however, prevent you from communicating with non-members. Users could contribute to bulletin boards within AOL's subscription services which extended its reach outside the United States. AOL first launched in Japan in 1986 and by the early 1990s had thousands of users across the world socially interacting with each other. CompuServe was a very popular service, topping more than 3 million users by 1995, whilst AOL provided online games for the Commodore from 1985 and a graphical chat environment from 1986.

Talking in real time
When you 'talk' to someone on a bulletin board, it's a bit like chatting using mobile phone text messages, and online users wanted something more like a conversation. This need was filled when Internet Relay Chat, was developed.

One of the first examples of news broadcasting using Internet Relay Chat was when it was used to report on the 1991 Soviet *coup d'état* attempt even though there was a media blackout in force at that time.[6] It was used in a similar fashion during the Gulf War, the 1992 US presidential election, and the Oklahoma City bombing in 1995. There are also some examples of weddings being conducted online there! I do wonder whether the happy couples are still married to each other or whether they have announced their separation in a similar community spirited fashion. The idea of Twitter broadcasting news events is certainly not a new concept at all.

As these different streams of communications evolved over time, it became apparent that there were disparate islands of information surrounded by a sea of data. These pieces of information weren't connected to each other at all. CompuServe and AOL forged ahead with their own communities, significantly growing users at a tremendous rate but creating an issue. The main problem with walled gardens is that if you want to interact with your friends who have accounts in other networks, you have to join the other network.

> Walled gardens require all of your contacts to use the same network in order to get value from the connection.

This closed type of interaction only brings benefits to the company that built the network software. Soon browsers such as Netscape circumvented the walled garden approach by providing the mechanism to visit websites around the world. Netscape used graphical user interfaces to present easy to navigate pages with images and files to download. Communication using Network News Transfer Protocol (NNTP) allowed forum software and newsreader software to proliferate, encouraging interaction between disparate members of the new Internet community. NNTP and newsreader software are still used by forum moderators, technical experts and regular contributors to this day. Their main benefit is that they allow offline responses to posted questions on myriad forums covering any topic you'd care to ask about.

Social and non-social software
Fifteen years ago, where did you go to get information about someone to get your work done? You probably tried the library, visited the bookstore, or looked in an encyclopaedia. The information you needed would be stored there and the data was as fresh as the day the book was sent to print. Now let's move forward to today. Where would you go to get that information? You'd go onto the web. Specifically, you'd use a search engine to find the information you need. Some of the data you'll find will be static, and some of the information will be dynamic, up to date and engaging. The web has changed into Web 2.0, it's changed the way you find the things you want and it's become much more interactive and social.

> The way that social media has been adopted is different from the way that other types of 'non-social' software have been used.

If you're working at your PC on desktop applications like Adobe Illustrator, Excel or Word, you do not require validation from your peers in your network or recommendations for you to use the software or find it valuable. You may have heard about the software from someone and decided to try it yourself. Non-social software started to change with the introduction of collaborative applications. Tools like SharePoint, Lotus Notes, Outlook and Instant Messenger introduce the concept of 'others' in your network. You can interact and collaborate with these 'others' in different ways. You can send an email which is instantly delivered or you can update a document on the network which can alert others in your workgroup that the document has changed. You can send an instant message to people across the company and communicate online with your team mates. Collaboration software enables you to interact with 'the others' to efficiently get your work done.

THE GROWTH OF THE WEB 2.0 WORLD

Web 2.0 and social networks exist and thrive because users communicate with each other. They engage in conversations with each other, commenting and responding to information on the web. The conversation started with email, bulletin boards, forums and newsgroups. Now you will probably update your Twitter status and you will talk about what you are doing on Facebook. You can comment on blogs, take a quick online survey or respond to a poll on a website. You can take notes during a webcast and store them online. All of this and more is possible with Web 2.0.

Web 2.0 is a term associated with web applications that allow user interaction.

These applications facilitate interaction, information sharing and collaboration amongst web based communities and social networking sites. For technology influencers, Web 2.0 is about the perpetual beta which is the shift in the way that web applications were developed and deployment. Interaction and feedback between the users and the software designers means that products can continually be updated as the product evolves. The traditional software design life cycle focuses on producing a software product, evaluating and testing it. The product is then launched and used by consumers who often have had no impact on any product design decisions. Web 2.0 allows feedback, interaction and change. Web 2.0 is about constantly changing the technology as people can give feedback on the process by interacting with the software designers and changing the development life cycle.

Consequently Web 2.0 changed the genre of applications. Now there are web applications focused on user centred design, there are sites designed for sharing and there are application mashups. A mashup is a web page or application that combines different sources of data in the form of a service. For example, real-time traffic data in one application can be merged with a mapping application and the merged application used to benefit travellers.

Letting the folks work for you

Web 2.0, with its interaction and dialogue, has brought interoperability and collaboration to the World Wide Web.

The term Web 2.0 is associated with Tim O'Reilly, who ran the O'Reilly Media Web 2.0 conference in 2004. This conference is credited with starting the discussion about the term Web 2.0 in the public forum and brought the idea of the collaborative web alive. Now new genres of services and applications have sprung up: video sharing sites, wikis, blogs, podcasts and forums. Formerly, in what is called the age of Web 1.0, we used static websites and were limited to clicking links to view other static websites. Now Web 2.0 allows users to interact with each other, rate content, edit web pages and modify the style of the page.

Web 2.0, which seemed to rise out of the ashes of the dotcom bubble, brought start-up websites with discussions and interaction between companies and their customers.

This type of interaction is completely different from the way we previously interacted with our friends. I used to use traditional ways of communicating like email and instant messaging to chat to my friends and colleagues. Whenever I found out something new or interesting, I'd send out the link or more probably an attachment to the email and send it to my group of friends. I used forum software to ask technical questions and discuss topics with the online community. Now, I share the link on Twitter or Facebook and I ask my extended network of friends if they have the answer to my questions. I use email distribution lists or forum software as a last resort. How times have changed – and social networking sites have enabled that change for me.

Documents can now be found when you search for terms that are relevant to **you**.

Users now decide how documents are classified or tagged on the web.

These tags, keywords relating to the document or web page, can be grouped together in a 'tag cloud'. A tag cloud is a collection of keywords on a web page indicating which keywords have been marked by more people as relevant descriptions of the document. These tag categories, where the same term was used by several people, started to rise in prominence in the form of tag clouds, where more popular tags appear in larger font sizes. Other users can then see which tag name has been classified by the largest number of community members and can use the new tag name. This collaboration encourages new forms of page grouping as the new type of user generated taxonomy emerges.

Figure 3.4 Tag cloud from my blog, http://eileenbrown.wordpress.com

The tag cloud in Figure 3.4 was taken from my blog at http://eileenbrown. wordpress.com. It's easy to see the sort of words I use more often than others in my recent blog entries.

There has been an increase in collaborative technologies that support real-time interactions and user-generated content. Instead of the traditional taxonomy we now have the concept of the folksonomy.

A folksonomy is something that is classified by 'the folks' instead of an unnamed project team who follow a formal structure for classifying documents.

Folksonomies started to appear as users' tagged content on web pages and assigned categories that were relevant to them. I might classify a topic on the web by a completely different term than you. For example, you might have tagged the story about the Icelandic volcano eruption as 'air travel disruption', whereas I might tag the same eruption as a 'pyroclastic flow'. Others may tag the same eruption with different terms.

This collaborative approach means that anyone can release a partially finished application onto the web, and due to the efforts and feedback of the many, the application can evolve with active participants throughout the development process. This is a fundamental shift in the way that large companies produce software. Their software development cycles were just not agile enough to cope with this level of interaction.

In the world of Web 2.0, applications are developed with massive amounts of input and collaboration from the online community.

With the potential for a whole world of beta testers collaborating with the application developer, the potential in the industry for disruption is huge. The development teams are now participants in an ongoing cyclical process in which the beta testers use the software and offer feedback. Now with careful co-ordination the developers can listen to feedback from their end users, ordinary folks like you and me. They can redesign and develop that software, improve it with iterations of the code, asking for feedback from people like us and bringing the software closer to the needs and requirements of the users.

SOCIALISING AND INTERACTING

For me, Web 2.0 has made socialising with my friends and business colleagues in my existing social networks much easier.

Web 2.0 interaction lets me connect to people outside my immediate network, to bring them closer to me in my social graph.

It also allows me to see what is going on in my second degree network, my friends of friends network. I can stay in touch with colleagues and partners with whom I only tend to work for a few weeks per year. I can find out what my business connections are working on at the moment, which gives me an opportunity to reconnect with them and remind them of my consultancy skills. Social tools such as Facebook, LinkedIn and Twitter allow me to see what the friends of my friends are saying. This makes me want to interact with these connections more frequently, enables me to extend my network and connect to networks outside my social graph.

Web 2.0 provides huge diversity in the way that products are showcased. The ability for organisations to disseminate information via text, video, slides and audio enhances learning in so many ways.

Companies in service industries can use the interaction for better customer dialogue.

Businesses can take advantage of this by providing educational blogs about products and services. The can record 'how to' videos to upload onto YouTube and they can publish audio podcasts for background details and education. Imagine what a revolution this could be for schools and colleges. Teachers could take advantage of the favoured method of learning and teach children using this new media. Pupils could become much more engaged and learning could be enhanced.

Some companies have externally facing wikis for customer comments and feedback on documents; others have forums for help and advice for customers. There are many sites dedicated to helping to educate visitors about medical issues and questions about their wellbeing. There are forums, Q&A documents, and there is even a YouTube channel called FlowTheBook, which is specifically designed for parents to help educate their daughters about menstruation. All of these sites are searchable; they are discoverable and they all give users the ability to interact with the site itself. These sites are much more useful than the medical dictionary sitting on your bookshelf gathering dust.

Creating your organisation's social graph
Some key decision makers and influencers in a network don't play an active part in online activities, but have huge impact throughout their networks.

> These influential decision makers are deep within an organisation and are the 'go to' people when there are problems.

They may be the ideas people when you need to brainstorm, and the people that you can rely on to complete complex tasks. They are valued contacts, trusted advisers, have the ear of the senior executives and are often the hubs of joined networks inside organisations and key to the social graph. These interpersonal ties carry information between people, they can be strong or weak, but they transmit across their networks. Unfortunately, companies don't often know who these valuable people are and waste time repeating work that might not be needed.

A social graph of your organisation, created either manually or using social graphing and mapping tools, can map the number of ties each individual has, whether weak or strong, and indicate which people within your organisation are central to its connectedness. Three or four questions could be asked and the answers mapped out graphically. If you have well connected people, the graph could look very much like a hub and spoke network diagram, or perhaps even a fully meshed network topology. For example, some of the questions that you could ask are:

> Your organisational social graph
>
> • Who do you go to within your company for reliable and accurate information?
> • Who would you trust to get a complex project completed?
> • Who helps you connect to the resource you need?

These graphs, once created, can potentially show a network hidden within your organisation which is totally different than the type of network that may be mapped out by the organisational structure. These charts don't map to hierarchy – far from it. Often middle managers and individual contributors who need to communicate and connect with multiple groups across an organisation, share information and disseminate information through their many communicated ties.

> Their relative importance to an organisation depends on the number of strong and weak ties they have.

Strong ties are people in your network with whom you have a good relationship. Weak ties are your casual acquaintances, people you know vaguely, but don't have a regular connection to.

Some people seem to know hundreds of people, albeit casually, whereas others have deeper relationships with fewer people. How do people manage these relationships? A recent posting on Facebook said: 'The human mind can only deal with about 200 close relationships. If you have more than 200 friends on Facebook it doesn't mean you are popular, it means your quality control is bad, or your ego is too big.'

There does appear to be a limit to the number of friends you can have. A British anthropologist, Robin Dunbar, hypothesised that there is a theoretical limit to the number of people with whom we can maintain stable social relationships. This number is set at 150. Tools such as Facebook allow you to greatly extend this number using weak ties.

YOUR STRONG AND WEAK TIES

Strong ties can guide you towards other strong networking hubs, and they tend to indicate powerful networks, with very well connected individuals at the hub.

> Unusual information tends to flow better between the weaker ties in your network.

Your strong ties probably have access to the same information that you have. These ties are in the same network as you are and they are less likely pass information around. This same information, however, may be news to the weaker ties in your organisation.

> People connected to you by weaker ties are more likely to propagate the information to people outside your network.

Some individuals are very well connected to other people who work in tightly connected groups like a network hub. These hubs have both strong and weak ties connecting them to other parts of the network. These routing hubs maintain relationships with key central characters and they keep the flow of information inside an organisation moving efficiently.

Mapping your organisation out in this way can identify potential communication issues within your organisation.

The mapping can often highlight positive connections and it can strengthen communications flow. Breaking down the disparate islands of information within an organisation by using either human connections or collaboration software such as email, a document management system or a wiki can improve the information flow within a company and streamline processes.

People hubs, routers and endpoints

To understand how social media can be of benefit inside the organisation, we need to look at how real networking works and why it is useful for some people and not others. To think about the human network, I'd like you to think about hardware hubs and routers. If you think about your circle of friends you'll notice that some people have a tendency to be natural hubs. These people have a collection of friends that feed them information and ask their advice. Other friends seem to behave as routers. These people don't often have the information you need when you ask them a question but they usually know someone who does. Others in your circle of friends are endpoints. They usually ask all the questions. So let's consider endpoints.

Endpoints (or nodes, if we're staying with the technology analogy) need information.

They often don't have connections to enough people in the workplace to be able to network efficiently and get the information they need. This is especially true in larger organisations. Endpoints tend to ask questions of hubs so that they can get the information they need. Sometimes they may need to be connected to others in the organisation that may be able to help.

Hubs tend to have lots and lots of connections in the organisation.

These connections might be strong ties or weak ties. There may be connections to several people throughout the network who can provide the answer to anyone who comes for information. If a hub doesn't have the answer directly, they will often know someone who does have the answer. This third party may be someone with whom the hub has an infrequent or casual relationship – a weak tie. Perhaps this connection may be someone whom the hub has only met once but recognises the potential value of the relationship and connects whenever they need to.

When a hub doesn't have the answer to the question, but knows someone else will be able help then the hub turns into a router.

35

Routers pass information onto other hubs to find the answer that they need.

An endpoint will sometimes find they connect to a hub, are passed through another hub (who may or may not have the answer) and on until the correct person is found. Hubs and routers are the best connected people inside an organisation, and endpoints might try to find out who their primary hubs are. Having a good strong connection with the hubs in your organisation is a great way to encourage effective knowledge flow. The best and strongest connections are between hubs and routers themselves. If we're still staying with the hardware and networking topology analogy, you might be thinking about a fully meshed diagram by now. These are the most valuable connections you can make. Are you a hub yourself? Are you a routing hub? I class myself as a routing hub. I have lots of connections that I maintain a relationship with and I often pass people onwards if I don't have the answer myself.

The only problem with this model is that endpoints often feel that they have nothing of value to offer a hub. Endpoints only seem to want information and they don't tend to contribute information to the network. Hubs and routers thrive on two-way information flow and will be reluctant to maintain two-way connections where they don't benefit from the relationship. Hubs and routers get the most value from other hubs and routers.

If you think you're an endpoint and want to grow your connections, how can you become a hub? I use the 'extra fact' to give out a hook.

When you start to connect with someone, try to give a little bit more information than you receive.

In an opening conversation when someone asks how you are – don't just say 'I'm fine, thank you'. Try to give a little bit of extra information to open up the conversation which will encourage dialogue with the other person. Perhaps you could say 'I'm fine, thank you, although I'm totally delighted to have completed the public folder phase and I'm now onto phase 2 of my Exchange migration project' (or something similar). This could potentially open up a dialogue about you as a person and your current project. Perhaps you might find another Exchange specialist in a pinstripe suit. The topic isn't all that important; engaging someone in conversation is.

Sharing a little personal information often opens up the dialogue and encourages the other person to interact with you. This starts your two-way conversation and starts to strengthen the tie. With your collections of new ties, strong and weak, you'll start to be a little hub – and your personal network inside the business will start to grow.

So what kind of tools should you use to communicate in the new world of engagement? Do you start with a blog, or do you start your own video channel? It seems overwhelming and it seems very transient. Should you bother at all and wait for this craze to go away?

SUMMARY

- Create an effective and comprehensive social media plan.
- Metrics really matter. Create a baseline and record metrics and measurements.
- Walled gardens need to connect to the outside world for the benefit of their users.
- Use folksonomies for a better understanding of how your customers classify things.
- Use social media interaction for better customer service opportunities.
- Create your organisation's social graph to find out who your internal influencers are.
- Work out who your hubs, routers and endpoints are.
- Use the 'extra fact' to get your hook.
- Cultivate your strong and your weak ties. Both are valuable.

4   THE TOOLS OF THE NEW WEB

Where do you start to get your message out in the new Web 2.0 world? Which applications, amongst the hundreds available, could you consider? In this chapter, we will start by looking at blogging and how a blog can help to start the conversation between you and your audience. We'll then look at how to consume information on a blog and the various tools you can use to read posts, both online and offline. We'll talk about editing your own web pages, and how wikis can be used as powerful tools both inside and outside the firewall. We'll move onto video and web conferencing software and how virtual meetings can be conducted across the web using low cost or free software. We'll talk about mobile blogging and microblogging, discuss the rise of Twitter and include some techniques to enhance your communication over 140 characters. Finally, we'll look at the other worlds – the virtual worlds that exist and the world of the online gamer – and explore how businesses can take advantage.

THE TOOLS OF WEB 2.0

Social computing tools are feature rich and powerful. They are diverse and help to solve a series of communications problems. They provide information to help connect people. Sites such as Ning and MySpace segregate communities into specialist areas, and blogs, wikis, forums and instant messaging applications enhance the interaction on the sites themselves. They propagate information by word of mouth networking and connections. They earn their revenue through paid-for advertising and sponsorship. They can be used to collate targeted groups. These sites can operate for professional purposes or purely for hobbyists. LinkedIn, which positions itself as a business networking site, is also a great source of job listings and a quick way of looking at candidates' curricula vitae and career histories. Other examples of such sites are Facebook, Bebo, Orkut, KickApps and Friendster.

Planning to incorporate these sites into your plan requires some discipline to manage the updates from each site effectively. Some networking sites have their own alerts built into the software which enable you to receive emails when certain actions are triggered. Part of your implementation plan might include allowing for appropriate timely action whenever an alert is generated.

Corporate blogging

One way that companies can start to communicate with their customers outside their formal public relations (PR) and communications mechanisms is by allowing their employees to broadcast their message to their customers through blogging.

Forward-thinking companies with fresh innovative ideas and good blogging policies in place experience a perception shift amongst their customers. Over time, after interaction with bloggers, customers discover that the company is staffed with real people with families, homes, a sense of humour and not mechanoids without a soul.

Blogging, the publishing of information to a web log, allows information and links to be published onto the web in a dynamic way. Your customers will read what you publish on your blog to get information and advice from you. Posts are published in reverse chronological order so that the latest post is shown at the top of the page. Your readers can add their comments to your blog entries, and other bloggers can link to your blog entry from their own blog.

The mechanism of cross-linking to a blog post on another blog is called a trackback or a pingback and it is a useful way for you to track who reads your content.

Subscribing to blogs

Your readers can subscribe to your blog using RSS. RSS stands for Really Simple Syndication – or Rich Site Summary, according to some site definitions – and is an essential tool for websites that have rapidly changing content. In order to take advantage of the RSS feature on a website, you need a feed reader, or aggregator. Subscribers of your blog consume RSS feeds through a feed aggregator. Offline readers such as Sharpreader and Newsgator allow you to read content when you are not connected to the Internet, or you can use a tool such as Google Reader to read aggregated content when you are online. There are also versions of RSS readers specifically designed for mobile devices. When you subscribe to an RSS feed on a web page, your feed reader periodically scans each URL that you have subscribed to, checks for updated content on the page and, if there is new content, downloads a copy for you to read later. The information also includes extra information in meta-tags, such as the date of publication and the owner of the post and a link back to the original post in case you want to add a comment to the post. The content is actually pulled from the URL by the reader itself although it appears to have been pushed to out to subscribers each time a new post is published or created by the author.

Due to the technical limitations of RSS, it isn't possible to obtain statistics on who is subscribing to your RSS feed, which may be an issue for you if your customer engagement strategy includes measuring specific metrics around subscriber types.

Blog syndication

Feed syndicator tools like Feedburner can keep track of your subscribers.

A feed syndicator allows material to be made available to many other websites and for you to measure each click. They can tell you how many unique new subscribers are reading your posts, which can be a useful mechanism if you need to track audience engagement.

Websites that have content that is updated from time to time should consider placing an RSS Feed button on their web page for users to subscribe to and receive push notifications. Hosted blog sites such as Blogger, Wordpress, TypePad, Joomla and Windows Live Spaces all have these feed notification buttons incorporated.

Business to business blogging

There are personal blogs, there are product blogs. There are corporate blogs, and there are blogs written by cats and dogs. Which one is the right approach? Microsoft has many different bloggers who talk about technology innovation, research, opinion and upcoming product releases. There are thousands of bloggers who blog as individuals, there are product team blogs, and support team blogs. There are blogs written on the main Microsoft sites of http://blogs.msdn.com and http://blogs.technet.com. There are blogs written using Live Spaces, Wordpress, LiveJournal and many more. There's a huge amount of information coming from inside the company, designed to educate, inform and announce news to Microsoft's partners and customers. Microsoft is a good example of B2B blogging. Credibility, authority and authenticity all help the customer or partner make an informed decision about Microsoft's large product set. With the huge amount of information flowing from Microsoft every day, it would not be feasible to aggregate all this information into one main channel. It may be possible for a small company to have one 'voice' when engaging with customers or partners, but for large companies this could not work. Would it even be possible for one blog account to aggregate all of the work people are doing in one company without the blog sounding like a PR message? Any major corporate announcement is generally tied to PR initiatives at a corporate level where perhaps there isn't a place on the website for comments from the readers of that message. With a carefully executed PR strategy around these announcements, and a good corporate policy in place, the voice of the blogger (and the microblogger) can be heard, and it can be a very powerful voice indeed when it is closely aligned with corporate strategy and an effective plan in place.

THE POWER OF COLLECTIVE HUMAN KNOWLEDGE

If the PR announcement generates excitement and buzz, and people want to find out more information about your product, new technique or news disclosure, they will go to your site for information. If the only place to go for information is the official press site, people may get frustrated at the lack of news other than the official PR release. Having an information channel such as a blog, populated by key people who have information and opinions, gives a human perspective to the PR announcement and encourages dialogue with the company. This leads to a perspective of greater transparency and honesty.

Companies that permit their staff to have a public voice and permit them to broadcast to the outside world through their blogs, often gain benefits from using similar forms of collaboration inside the company. There is a wealth of collaboration tools available for use inside the company network. There are applications with embedded presence for instant updates, alerts for document changes and broadcasts, and collaborative applications such as internal wikis. Collaboration tools like these can ensure that companies can effectively share their intellectual property (IP) safely inside their network boundary and behind their security firewall. Staff realise that often some of the simplest ways for teams to collaborate is through the use of team wikis.

Wikis are a great way to get interaction from customers and partners. Wikipedia, a website which contains over 15 million articles, is a wiki. It can be edited and added to by anyone who wishes to modify details on a page. It is imperative that corporate entities have a presence on Wikipedia giving information about the company. If your company is global, then there is a further opportunity for you to reach customers across the non-English-speaking world by localising versions of the corporate page. Almost 80% of articles in Wikipedia are written in languages other than English. For example, the BCS (search for "British Computer Society" in Wikipedia) has its own page. The page includes history, membership details, and certification and there are links to regional BCS branches throughout the UK.

Wikis, by their design, are made to be edited. Unfortunately, some careless editing of a page may do considerable damage to the body of work already created. This damage, whether intentional or otherwise, means that there needs to be some kind of alert mechanism in place to prevent destruction of work already completed. Wikipedia does have a huge problem with wiki editing, both from reporting of inaccurate information, and people deliberately or otherwise falsifying Wikipedia entries. This malicious editing is termed wiki vandalism. Wikipedia defines vandalism as:

> Removing all or significant parts of a page's content without any reason, or replacing entire pages with nonsense. Sometimes referenced information or important verifiable references are deleted with no valid reason(s) given in the summary. ... An example of blanking edits that could be legitimate would be edits that blank all or part of a biography of a living person.[7]

Some wiki vandalism is difficult to discover, however. False or misleading information in a regular technical document on your intranet may escape detection. This information will probably be plausible. It may appear to be true but is deliberately designed to obfuscate the true meaning. Misinformation like this could lead to significant issues with knowledge transfers within the company, especially if the mistake has been made deliberately. There must be an effective way to track who is using the wiki, what changes are being made, and by whom. An audit trail is an effective way of recovering your data, especially if an effective alerting system is used. This becomes even more critical when that wiki information is on a site posted on your externally facing website and could be compromised by anyone. In this case, an effective alerts strategy, coupled with proactive monitoring of the site and an effective rollback policy for wiki pages, will alleviate any concerns about unscrupulous vandalism.

To make effective connections with your audience it is important to monitor your feeds and respond to your customers' concerns and comments. Setting alerts on blogs, so that you receive an email every time anyone posts a comment on an entry, will enable you to be responsive. This is good PR for the person who posted the original comment, but it also helps to stop your site being spammed by any bots that are using your blog to draw attention to their own blog. These automated blogs typically exist to drive traffic to their own site, and associated advertisements, and they place a link on your blog in the form of a trackback or link in a comment. These links are used by Google as a measure of how popular these external sites are, and are used to increase the page rank of that site. Again, having an effective alert process in place will enable you to remove the links to these sites before the web crawlers have indexed the site and artificially inflated their site popularity rankings.

TOOLS, TOOLS, TOOLS

Terms and concepts

Outside the firewall, blogs and wikis are just one part of the digital engagement toolset. There are many other tools:

TOOLS AND TERMS

- **Podcast** A digital media file, typically audio, made available for download from a website in a consistent format.
- **Vlogging** Short for 'video blogging', which delivers video or Internet television from blogs and from video sharing sites such as YouTube.
- **Moblogging** A mechanism allowing blog posts to be published from a mobile phone.
- **Phlogging** Short for 'photo blogging', where photos are uploaded from a mobile phone directly to the web for sharing.
- **Screencast** A recording of a computer screen, perhaps showing a demonstration of a feature which is captured in video format using a capture tool and uploaded to the web.

These tools, and many more like them, add to the wealth of news distribution mechanisms which encourage user generated content to be added to the web. With an effective plan for finding your customers, engaging with them and getting them to become advocates for your brand, you can leverage these Web 2.0 tools to your advantage and enhance your business.

There are so many tools to update your networking sites that it could take an age to go through them all to update them. Fortunately, there are information aggregators that allow you to pool relevant information. Some tools, Huddle for example, work well for online collaborative ventures or create online workspaces for virtual team work. Other tools, such as Digg, Reddit and Stumbleupon, relay content, news and information, keeping followers up to date. Some tools like Hunch and Yelp in the US are rating services for people to give feedback on a product or a service, and others like Google Reader are online personal aggregators of news. All of these sites are designed to make things easier to find on the social web, linking videos, blogs and other websites together in one useful place, ready to be tagged, marked as a favourite and commented upon by community.

Video
The value of meeting someone face to face cannot be underestimated if you want to be successful in business. However, there are alternatives such as talking to customers on the telephone or seeing them online. There are many applications available on the web that do this – both for consumers and corporates – and they help people communicate wherever they are. Voice over Internet protocol (VoIP) and a headset together enable seamless audio and video communication from computer to computer. All you need is a computer with audio and a webcam. Popular applications include Adobe Acrobat Connect, GoogleTalk, iChat, Intercall, Meetcam, Microsoft Live Meeting, Radvision, Stickam, Skype, Telepresence, WebEx and Yahoo! Messenger.

Blogs
Blogs are personal, compelling and can be hugely successful in a very short space of time. You can find blogs on almost any topic you care to name.

For example, Judith O'Reilly writes the Wife in the North blog.[8] Judith only started to blog when her husband, who wanted to bring up her children in a country setting away from London, moved the family to Northumberland, 30 minutes from the nearest town. Her husband was kept in London for weeks at a time with his work, so Judith started to blog in 2006 as a way of chronicling how different and challenging her new life was.

Her blog is notable for how quickly she managed to turn her blog into a book deal. Her blog was linked to by Tom Watson MP, an influential parliamentary blogger. Tom's blog was linked to by Iain Dale, another influential blogger. Iain's blog was commented upon by Andrew Sullivan, a writer and columnist. The comment came to the attention of Patrick Walsh, a literary agent based in the UK, who contacted Judith about a book deal. This is a classic example of how effective the word of mouth network can be in getting your message out. Judith was amazed by the attention. She wrote:[9]

> Blogging is a strange and wonderful thing. I reached out into cyberspace because I needed to – not in any expectation of a book deal. Better than a book deal, any book deal, have been the kindly comments, e-mails and messages from strangers who aren't strangers any more who said: 'I read you and you made me laugh' and 'I read you and you made me cry'. My book deal isn't so much about money; it is more to do with the fact that blogging is a force to be reckoned with. Ultimately blogging is people willing to commit time, effort and emotion.

Mobile blogging

Moblogging, which is the ability to blog, upload videos or pictures from your mobile phone, has grown significantly over the past few years.

> The ability to microblog, or use short status updates, post photos or videos, makes the moblogging concept compelling to the consumer and gives companies a great marketing opportunity to connect at the actual event.

Mobile blogging is popular with tourists, people on the move or people who want to post blog entries as they are happening. The ability to communicate with others at events, posting images of new announcements or items, shows readers what you are seeing at the time you are seeing it. You can post updates to your blog, upload photos, sound bites or video clips whilst you are actually at the event watching the news unfold. You are effectively blogging 'live'.

With the advent of applications for mobile phones such as Twitter and Facebook and location aware applications, you can automatically update your location from your device. This term has evolved to include any status update, image or video update from a mobile device or smart phone.

Microblogging: the shorter blog

Microblogging is defined as a shortened version of blogging, uploading an image or posting a video to a website. The most notable microblogging sites are Tumblr, Plurk, Yammer and Twitter, which has exploded in popularity since its launch in April 2006. More and more business is being conducted online, so the value of Twitter cannot be underestimated. With around 50 million status messages or tweets per day according to the Twitter blog, someone, somewhere, is listening to what you have to say. It's a hugely powerful way of promoting your business, connecting with your customers and creating buzz about your brand. With Twitter, you have up to 140 characters to create and post your message, which is then broadcast to the world. Anyone can follow you without your consent. Everything you tweet appears on your feed stream and anyone can click on the link to follow your status updates. If you want to build privacy into your status updates you can. You can decide to protect your updates so that they can't be seen by everyone. Then, when someone wants to follow you on Twitter, you can decide to permit them to follow you. Therefore only people you have individually authorised can see your Twitter stream.

It's very easy to get started on Twitter. All you need to do is to set up a profile and a unique user name on the site. The user name is used in the URL and takes the form of http://twitter.com/username. No spaces or characters other than underscores are permitted in the name. Users communicate with you directly by including your Twitter username, preceded by the '@' sign in their message, which is called a tweet. This message can be seen by anyone who follows the sender of the original message, so whole conversations can be followed. To privately send a tweet which can be seen by the recipient only you need to precede the tweet by the letter D. This is known as a direct message or DM.

You can customise your profile with extra information about yourself within the 160 character limit which is more than the 140 characters permitted by each Twitter status update. You can upload a photo and include a link to your website or blog. You build lists to group people into categories which can be seen by any-one who sees your profile. You can 'favourite' a particular tweet for your reference. This status message which can also be seen by others if they click on your favourites button on your page. You can tag topics by using a hashtag. A hashtag is a word preceded by the character # which can be searched for. If many people use the same hashtag, it can become a trend for others to use. The search func-tion in Twitter lets you search for phrases, words, hashtags or people.

The retweet
The most powerful mechanism is the art of the retweet. A retweet is when some-one rebroadcasts your original status update to their own followers, amplifying your message. There are three main things you need to think about when you planning a message and want it to be retweeted:

User names:
My own Twitter user name, @eileenb, is eight characters in length out of the available maximum of 140 characters. If I want to create something compelling in my status update to engage the audience and encourage a series of retweets then I need to consider this:

HOW TO GET YOUR STATUS RETWEETED

- I want to make sure that, when my message is rebroadcast, the context of the original message isn't lost. Therefore I need to make sure that my original message is short enough to be rebroadcast.

- The first few characters of my message when it is retweeted by another person looks like this: RT @eileenb. This phrase is 12 characters in length. I've counted one trailing space after the character 'b' for spacing purposes. This gives me 128 remaining characters to create my original message.

- Most third party Twitter clients use the form 'RT' at the start of the message, but that's not the only option available. Some seasoned Twitter users use the term 'via'. However, `via' uses another character from my allocation and would leave only 127 characters for the message.

This is something to keep in mind when you're planning the update that you want to have retweeted. But what if you intend your message to be broadcast over and over again?

Multiple retweets:
Suppose your carefully crafted message, consisting of a maximum of 124 characters, gets retweeted and the news is so interesting that it gets retweeted again. A retweet appends a further name to the tweet which now looks like this: RT@eileenb @quiggles. This new format uses 22 characters from your original allocation of 140, including the trailing space. The more retweets you get, the more user names are appended to the message, leaving fewer characters for the actual message.

URL shorteners:
Try not to put a shortened URL at the end of your tweet. You may be well within your 140-character limit with the original tweet but after it's been retweeted twice without care, the last few characters may have disappeared from the URL, which could leave you with a URL that looks like

http://tinyurl.com/ydr

instead of the five or six characters you actually need to visit the destination page.

Getting your message rebroadcast
People buy from people and relationships do matter, even if they are relationships that started in 140-character form. Getting people to talk about you is important – as are referrals and retweets. Retweets are a great way of getting the message across and amplifying it throughout the Twitter audience. You'll never get poor content rebroadcast, so it's important to consider the impact of your message and its newsworthiness. Make sure you retweet other interesting pieces of information that you find to propagate to your own followers.

There is an awful lot of 'noise' on Twitter, and it is estimated that out of over 10 million users, only 5% of these accounts are actively posting updates. The average tweet per user is 1, which indicates a large number of unused accounts. Statistics currently show that over 50% of accounts are completely inactive. Your challenge is how to channel the relationship that you have created with your Twitter followers into something worthwhile for your business. It is important to remember that Twitter is like any other communications channel. Make your users feel valuable by responding to them, rebroadcasting their messages and giving them more visibility which will encourage positive responses from them. Asking for help often brings new and valuable connections you hadn't considered before. I have discovered new friends on Twitter. I have been at events and total strangers have introduced themselves to me. They have followed me on Twitter and, due to my friendly style of interaction, they feel they know me personally. When I announce that I'll be at an event and will be at a certain place at a specified time, my virtual friends come and say hello. This turns my existing virtual relationship into a face to face relationship and strengthens bonds. I was at a trade show a couple of years ago and a man walked up to me extending his hand. 'Hi, I'm Gary', he said. I looked puzzled. 'Quiggles!' he announced. It was really great for me to meet someone with whom I'd been having a conversation for months but had never met.

Of course, with the huge amount of information flowing from Twitter, you need a client application to manage the people you follow and the messages they send. The most popular client application at the moment is Tweetdeck, although other applications like Twhirl and Hootsuite are popular. Applications for mobile devices like Twitterific, Twitterfon and Dabr help you tweet on the move. New applications appear and disappear regularly, so it's always a good idea to see what's hot or not at the moment.

VIRTUAL WORLDS AND GAMING

Large corporations such as Disney, Dell and Coca-Cola have a significant presence within virtual worlds because where users congregate there is an opportunity to do business. There are many forms of virtual worlds. There are worlds where you adopt an online identity and communicate with other users in an online environment whom you may or may not know. There are virtual online worlds like Second Life and World of Warcraft. Second Life enables its users to create a virtual identity and interact with other virtual identities with avatars in an online world.

Businesses have taken the example of user participation in these virtual worlds and have created online environments to engage users further. In Second Life, Apple has created an online store, while Microsoft has created virtual properties and theatres hosting online events. Sun has created a virtual campus for training its staff, and the BBC has hosted virtual music festivals.

Gaming and social interaction sites have a naturally symbiotic relationship that companies can leverage to engage their audience. Similar to virtual worlds, gaming environments feature altruistic games. In Facebook the Farmville MMORPG encourages players to give gifts to their farming neighbours and help out on their neighbours' farms. Co-operating in this way gives the player more experience points and helps them advance through the game. There are competitive MMORPG games such as Halo3, EverQuest and the World of Warcraft. In EverQuest, players participate in specific roles and collaborate with each other to win challenges. Pizza Hut has a business presence in the EverQuest game. All players need to do is type the command "/pizza" whilst they are playing EverQuest II. From within the game, the Pizza Hut website appears so that players can place an order for pizza whilst still playing the game. Companies that provide in-game adverts are not new in these types of online games, but this is the first example of being able to order a real pizza from a virtual world. Gamers don't mind these adverts either. Over 90% of gamers believe that real adverts add realism to the online game. The challenge for the advertiser, though, is that the players, on seeing the same adverts over and over again, soon begin to ignore them. New mechanisms that rotate adverts based on time of day are now being developed.

Even Twitter applications have appeared on the gaming scene. MMORPGs are hugely popular, as the millions of people who play Farmville, Mafia Wars and FishVille would testify. There is an in-game Twitter client for the World of Warcraft game called TweetCraft. World of Warcraft is the fastest selling PC game of all time, with millions of subscribers paying a monthly subscription of around $20. TweetCraft sends and receives messages from Twitter and Twitpic, and the Warcraft add-on receives messages from Twitter.

This collaboration between separate games enhances both of the applications. The ability to send and receive tweets whilst playing a game of World of Warcraft, upload screenshots of your game using TwitPic (a photo sharing site) and auto-matically post tweets about your achievements enhances the game and brings the community on board. You can also use a service such as Steam to digitally down-load games from the Internet, play and collaborate in an online community and engage with each other player socially. This many to many communications mech-anism is similar to that which allows Facebook to encourage gamers to see their friends recent gaming activity. Players can view their friends' groups, achieve-ments and games purchased. This friend network encourages gamers to try new games purchased by their online buddies, adding to Steam's revenue stream.

With the massive and varied choice of applications around, which one should you choose for your business? Should you create your own network for your hobby or join an established group? How many social media sites are there to engage in? What are they used for? Which site is suitable for you in your work, your home life or useful in your thirst for knowledge? Is there really a social networking site for everything imaginable?

SUMMARY

- There are many social media tools. Take time to choose the right ones for your business.
- Business to business blogging is vital to show your credibility, capability and authenticity.
- Use syndication to reduce your workload.
- Consider an external wiki to get input from the community.
- Use video sharing sites for 'how to' videos.
- Use microblogging for short impactful status messages.
- Try to create compelling content that gets retweeted.
- Consider the use of virtual worlds – wherever users congregate online there is an opportunity to do business.

5   NETWORKS

In this chapter we'll talk about some of the other main online interaction sites used for business, community, friends and family. We'll look at hobby sites, location sites and music streaming sites. We'll talk about online classified ad sites which enable you to find almost anything online, we'll talk about how you can buy and sell items. Twitter, the current darling of the digital conversation, has become the news hub of the moment, and we'll try to understand why this is. Finally, we'll look at how Generation Y is changing the way we work and how the way we interact is changing the way companies work. We'll start to look brand strategy and where you can start the conversation and collaboration with your customers.

A SITE FOR EVERY PURPOSE

Wherever you look there appear to be sites for connecting and engaging, yet I've only mentioned a few so far. Instead of researching an exhaustive list containing every different online interaction site I can find, I'll talk about a few. I've grouped some of the more popular online interaction sites below into the types of activities that they tend to be used for. This list isn't exhaustive, however; there are thousands of social networking sites, and the list is changing all the time. Wikipedia has a more comprehensive list and the main countries where these sites are popular, but it too is out of date. Here are the main popular sites at the moment.

Business networks
LinkedIn, with over 55 million registered users throughout the world, is considered the premier business networking site. There are opportunities to get introduced to new connections through your existing network, look for a job, or ask questions from industry experts. These connections can consist of your direct connections, their connections (your second degree connections) and their connections (your third degree connections). LinkedIn is mainly used to find jobs, to recommend others in your network and receive recommendations for your work. Recommendations on your profile are useful if you're looking for a new Recruiters and potential employers use these recommendations to determine how many people have recommended you, and they use the details on your profile to gauge your suitability for a role.

Ecademy is a business community founded in 1998 and claims to have 'millions of users'. It enables business people to connect through online networking. It uses connections from its membership to invite its members to business networking events and offers one to one meetings between its users. It offers a community that connects, refers and helps one another.

Xing is a business network with over 8 million members. Users connect using the six degrees of separation theory and have the ability to view upcoming events and search for other members. Like other networks, Xing allows them to advertise their skills and request connections across the site.

Ryze has over 500,000 members in specialist groups. It advertises the fact that members can 'rise up' through quality business networking. The site offers interaction, the chance to make connections and grow your networks. It offers networks on topics as diverse as 'A joke a day', 'Women in Networking' and 'MLM (Multi Level Marketing) for serious Network Marketers'.

Community
Ning is a site dedicated to building your own online community site where your users can congregate. These customised sites can be used for social clubs, committees, leisure activities and hobbyist sites. There are options to customise your site and to make it individual and eye-catching for your visitors.

Mumsnet is a site designed for parents. Anyone with children can register on the site and discuss parenting, childcare, contraception and issues of the day. In the run up to the 2010 general election in the UK, each political party was invited to answer questions on the site. Topics ranged from what each party's manifesto for mothers would be to what specific benefits for childcare they could expect to see with the new government.

Friends and family
Facebook, with over 600 million users, is a huge social site for personal and business use. It was initially used as a closed network within a walled garden for students at US universities, but the site was subsequently opened to all in 2005. It categorises users into different networks which can be towns, workplaces, companies or schools. Facebook has a huge number of applications written by developers to enhance the social nature of the site, using games quizzes and other methods to engage. Many companies use Facebook pages for business.

Bebo ('blog early blog often') is a social networking site which has been adopted by younger teens and children to socialise with their friends. They can customise their profiles with modules, quizzes and groups, with the opportunity to include a lifestream platform and timeline. A lifestream is a collection of items uploaded to the site and displayed in chronological order. Items can include video, photos, blog entries, notes and links. Bebo takes the privacy of its users very seriously and subscribes to Internet safety initiatives for children.

Friendster was created in 2002 and was an early attempt to connect friends and family together. It enabled you to meet new people by connecting to the friends of your friends, thereby taking advantage of the second degree network to extend your own circle of friends. It was initially designed to be an online dating site, but there was a rise in people who created fake identities on the site. This increase in 'fakesters' destroyed the ability to effectively connect real people using their social graph. Its popularity has waned in the US, but the site is still growing in Asia and has almost 120 million users.

Hi5 is a popular site for people to connect mainly in Latin America. It allows users to create an online profile, share photos and set up music streams on their profile.

Orkut, which is owned by Google, is very popular in Latin America and especially in Brazil. It is also very popular in India, but less so around the rest of the world. The site can be customised with themes to reflect particular tastes, you can add videos to your profile and employ a ranking scheme to grade your friends on a popularity scale. Orkut has had issues with spam applications in the past, and has been banned in some countries due to the lack of privacy controls, particularly over photos of women and concerns over ethical issues.

Hobby
Shelfari is a site dedicated to book lovers. It is owned by Amazon and allows users to build virtual bookshelves of the books they love. Shelfari allows bibliophiles to engage in discussions with other users and make recommendations on books to read.

Knowledge
Wikipedia is the epitome of social media concepts where the collective knowledge of the community is freely given to benefit all. Wikipedia started in 2001, and thousands of contributors have created a changing encyclopaedia. This dynamic online book is used by over 340 million people per month and is the fifth most read website in the world. There are over 13 million articles, 78% of which are written in languages other than English. The non-profit organisation is supported entirely by donations from its users who, in 2009, gave over $7.5 million to keep the infrastructure running and to try and maintain free access 'to the sum of all human knowledge'.[10]

Location
Foursquare is the current mobile device darling for announcing where you are. It operates in a similar way to Brightkite and Gowalla, which are also location announcing applications designed for mobile devices. It offers location based status updates for you to record the places you have visited. It also offers the opportunity to upload photos from that location and comment on the site. Friends can then receive alerts about your location. Identi.ca also allows you to upload microblog status updates from wherever you are.

Music
MySpace is a very popular site frequented by Generation Y and Z, and with musicians. Musicians have the ability to upload their entire catalogue of songs for download as MP3 files and to create playlists of their songs. Artists like Lilly Allen and Sean Kingston were initially discovered on MySpace, and many more have come to prominence from this site. The site appeals to teens and young adults due to the ability to heavily customise their profiles and their online page which is organised and used like a bedroom. This flexibility has kept MySpace popular with

Generation Y and Z despite the growth of Facebook – which has an interface which is much less customisable.

Last.fm is a music streaming site which recommends music according to your personal tastes. If you flag that you like a particular singer, then other songs from singers of a similar genre will be streamed to you. Any song you don't like will be removed from your individual playlist and there are opportunities to share your favourite music with others in your network by tagging your songs.

Updates
Plurk is a Twitter-like microblogging tool which shows user timelines and conversation history. It allows you to set your mood and track your followers' moods also. It is popular in Asia, but less so in Europe and the US.

There are thousands more of these sites, covering every genre imaginable. With the perpetual beta of Web 2.0, new sites pop up weekly and less popular sites fade from prominence. There are some sites that seem to have withstood the test of time. These sites cater for our primary business needs. Buying and selling things.

CLASSIFIEDS

When it comes to information, education and things to purchase, you can find just about everything on the Internet. There are directory sites pointing to other interesting websites, sites that sell and sites that advertise. But apart from huge, direct selling sites like Amazon, where do you go for classified ads, the sort that you find in the back of your local paper?

Craigslist is an online classified advertisement site that began in 1995 when Craig Newmark started to email his friends in the San Francisco area about local events. People placed paid adverts onto the site covering myriad products and services, including personal ads and adult services. It's now ranked 30th in the world in terms of page views per month, which is surprising for a site with such a simple design (see Figure 5.1). It has no images and allows minimal web page customisation and it now spans over 60 countries and over 700 regions.

Word of mouth about these local events ensured that both Craigslist subscribers and postings grew quickly. Craigslist soon also began to carry postings about job vacancies and small ads, which led to new categories being created. Unfortunately, lack of moderation on the site led to some underhand activities such as robbery, rape and murder.[11]

As Craig Newmark says, Craigslist works because it gives people a voice, a sense of community trust and even intimacy. Consistency of down-to-earth values, customer service and simplicity are also important.[12] But, there are always people who will use these networks for their own, not necessarily honourable means.

In addition to the usual definition of classified advertisements, there is also the concept of bidding for a product on auction sites. The market leader here is eBay,

Figure 5.1 Craigslist classified advertising site

which has listings advertising almost everything you can think of. The success of eBay from a reputational point of view is that you can read feedback about the seller by the buyer of the item. This fosters a sense of community amongst the buyers. If one buyer criticises the seller, the seller's reputation falls below 100% and never recovers. All feedback remains permanently attached to the seller's profile, along with a list of items that the seller has sold or purchased.

Some of the items for sale turn out to be much more successful than originally anticipated, or are sold at inflated prices as a result of viral notoriety.

Viral notoriety
Amusing or strange items for sale are often emailed around the Internet, adding to their notoriety and ultimately their saleability. This phenomenon has produced a new challenge. Some sellers will post a picture of the item for sale, with the naked image of the photographer in the photograph.[13] Reflectoporn, as it has come to be known, is where a person takes a photograph of a reflective object, such as a kettle or cutlery, while they are naked. Their image appears in the reflection of the item. The seller then puts this item up for sale on eBay with the photo to accompany it.[14] The link to the eBay item is then forwarded around the web virally. Other items spread virally due to their comedic nature. I remember a forwarded email with a link to an eBay wedding dress. A man modelled his ex-wife's wedding dress and included several photos of him wearing the dress complete with ponytail, beard and t-shirt. He explained that he was 'selling it hoping to get enough money for maybe a couple of Mariners tickets and some beer.' The $1200 dress sold for $3850.

Another eBay item which spread virally across the Internet was the Haunted Painting[15] which was viewed over 30,000 times in February 2000. According to the seller, the painting carried a form of curse. The description on eBay claimed that the characters in the painting moved during the night, and that they would sometimes leave the painting and enter the room in which it was being displayed. News of the listing was spread virally by Internet users who forwarded the link to their friends or wrote their own pages about it. Some people claimed that simply viewing the photos of the painting made them feel ill or have unpleasant experiences. Reports included people claiming to be violently ill or fainting, children screaming upon seeing the painting and observers were said to be gripped by an 'unseen entity'. Bidding began at $199 and the painting was sold for $1025.

So notoriety and visibility do seem to enhance sales. And notoriety, as the wedding dress seller discovered, can inflate the price far beyond anything originally anticipated.

THE INSTANT NEWS CHANNEL

Twitter seems to have evolved to being at the centre of news. It's a real-time hub where there are opportunities for sharing of information, news and media from any other social media source, whether it be a YouTube video, photos from a shared photo site, a link to comments or a new post on a blog. Everyone can propagate information, news and stories within moments and the man on the street can broadcast a story that spreads around the world in a flash. Everyone has a voice on Twitter and, joined together, it's a really powerful voice. The power of the crowd is enormous. People can create their own news.

Take for example, the Trafigura news story. In 2009, the *Guardian* newspaper in the UK claimed to have conclusive proof that toxic waste had been released in Côte d'Ivoire and reported that it had been prevented from covering remarks made in Parliament. Guido Fawkes, a political blogger, speculated that this injunction was linked to the Trafigura case. Although there was a news blackout in the UK, the Twitter community ensured that the story remained current, topical and at the forefront of news. Trafigura became a trending topic on Twitter, with thousands of messages all tagged with the hashtag #Trafigura. The gagging order on the *Guardian* was lifted the next day and the paper confirmed that Trafigura had been the source of the order.

This is really significant. Every member of the community has the ability to become a broadcaster and a commentator on the news.

The broadcaster gains credibility with their audience. Writers build relationships with their readers and the interaction between the newscaster and the readers becomes more personal.

Often people don't initially see the value of Twitter. They don't see the benefit of the real-time interaction with a huge potential audience. One of my friends, James, could not understand why people used Twitter at all. He felt that it was a stream of constant chatter distracting him from his day job. Now Twitter keeps him in touch with some of the key influencers in his industry, and he can have a useful dialogue with them on a far more regular basis than just at PR and industry events.

Twitter and Facebook can be linked together with status updates from Twitter appearing on Facebook and vice versa. Twitter has also integrated with LinkedIn so that status messages from Twitter appear on the feed at LinkedIn. The bringing together of parts of the Web 2.0 world in this way means that the edges of the worlds of each conversational tool are starting to blur more and more. These applications are no longer used in isolation, and this symbiotic relationship brings benefits on all sides.

But is Twitter leading or trailing edge? Does Twitter make the news, or just amplify some of the messages made by the few leading edge influencers on Twitter? Is **any** news broadcast mechanism leading edge? Or are we all just avid consumers and followers of the news? This news could be any type of information which happens to be reported by a Twitter user and comes to prominence as more and more people refer to the item so that it becomes a trend?

When you need to find out what's happening, where do you go? You probably don't pick up the newspapers, which might have been printed 18 hours earlier. Do you turn on the TV? Or do you listen to the radio? You will find out the news from your trusted advisers and they, very likely, will have got their information from the instant news channel – Twitter. Time and time again Twitter has had information and pictures about world events long before any other news channel has been able to begin broadcasting. When it comes to emergencies, Twitter seems to be quicker at disseminating information than the popular media channels. In the Australian bush fires in February 2009, the Australian fire authority sent out alerts using Twitter. In Mumbai in 2008, Twitter users helped to compile a list of the dead and injured during the attacks and announced locations where volunteers could go to donate blood.

Images uploaded to the web from a mobile device are also used to very powerful effect. In 2009, US Airways flight 1549, which had just taken off from New York's LaGuardia Airport, experienced a bird strike. The plane had to land on the Hudson River, which was a fairly routine simulator exercise for the pilot to do. News propagated around the world fairly quickly. The plane landed at 3.31 p.m.; within 6 minutes it was being reported in blogs and tweets, and images were being uploaded to photo sharing sites on the web (Figure 5.2). The time in the image below, shows the local time on, my computer and not the local time where the plane landed.

Photo sharing sites such as Flickr, YFrog and Twitpic, which permit the uploading of photos from mobile devices, guarantee worldwide transmission of images and on the spot access to eyewitness accounts. In an hour or so, more than one hundred pages of Twitter messages about the crash were generated and accessed by newsfeeds around the world. By the time the TV cameras and crews arrived, the passengers were being rescued and the plane was being moved to the jetty. I was looking at Twitter watching the news unfold in text and images. Where were you?

Figure 5.2 Tweet about the plane landing on the Hudson River

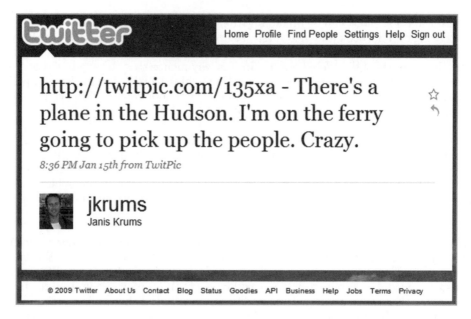

When J.F. Kennedy was shot, the world held its breath watching the grainy footage of the last few moments of his life. This 8mm film was shot by an amateur who was watching the motorcade. This footage was played over and over again as experts tried to analyse where the bullet came from. When Elvis Presley died in 1977, the world was informed by an official press release which hit the newspapers and TV some time later. His LP records immediately rushed to the top of the charts. When Michael Jackson was rushed into hospital at 1.14 p.m. on 25 June 2009 with suspected cardiac arrest, the news didn't trickle out from normal media channels. Community generated news site TMZ, which relies on 'hot tips', news snippets and images uploaded by its readers, was the first to break the news – well ahead of any traditional media outlets with reporters and paparazzi. This information spread around Twitter at an unprecedented rate. Biz Stone, co-founder of Twitter, said: 'We saw an instant doubling of tweets per second the moment the story broke. It is the biggest jump in tweets per second since the U.S. presidential election.'[16] By 10.30 p.m., tweets containing the words 'Michael Jackson' accounted for approximately 12% of all Twitter traffic (Figure 5.3), and there were so many requests for 'Michael Jackson' on Google that it was deemed by Google to be a denial of service attack.

Hundreds of memorial sites soon appeared across the Web and on Facebook. His albums rocketed straight to the top of the charts, and the film of his rehearsals for his concert zoomed into the top 10 movies within days. Michael Jackson's death, occurring in the glare of the beady eye of Twitter and the digital spotlight, has ensured that his star status will not fade for some considerable time yet.

Figure 5.3 Comment on Michael Jackson dominating Twitter traffic[17]

> ## My twitter search script sees roughly 15% of all posts on Twitter mentioning Michael Jackson. Never saw Iran or swine flu reach over 5%
>
> *11:03 PM Jun 25th from web*
>
> **EthanZ**
> Ethan Zuckerman

SOCIAL NETWORKS AND THE YOUNGER GENERATION

Generation Y is changing the way we work. Their ability to engage with multiple streams of communication, tools and websites and ably deal with the fire hose of information flooding at them will define our future working patterns. Generation Y thinks email is *passé* and tends not to use it. Generation Y graduates are moving into fast track management. They will be the next leaders of business and industry. Their current ways of working will become the new way of working for the baby boomer generation and Generation X – whether they like it or not.

Different online networking sites tend to be populated by different age groups. Teenagers and young adults tend to focus their attention on MySpace, Facebook, Bebo and Piczo. Adults of all ages now use Facebook for social and business purposes. The largest growth sector on Facebook is currently women in the 55–65 age range. Teenagers use these types of sites to network and form social groups with those in their peer group.[18] They join subgroups and share information among their friends.

TEENAGERS' BEHAVIOUR ON SOCIAL NETWORKING SITES

- Teenagers heavily customise their online profile as it is an easy way for them to express themselves.
- They update their profile and modify their status and other information regularly. They do this as an extension of their personality in much the same way as they will customise their bedroom.
- Their profile names are adorned with non-alphanumeric characters.
- They have mashups of media associated with their profile and the text in the 'about me' section changes frequently.
- Teenagers' online profiles are used as an extension of their status updates and their online identities.

This is a completely different form the way Generation X and older people use their profiles on these types of sites.

But why is this important in business? It's important to have a good understanding of how Generation Y and Z behave on social networking sites, and how they use their profiles, mobility and connections to live their digital life. Knowing these behaviour patterns gives you a great opportunity to effectively tune your social media architecture so that you can attract the correct audience to the right place. If your product sells to the young, then marketing your product in a way that is attractive to the young will give you credibility in their world and a positive return on your sales and marketing investment.

Have you considered your community and digital online conversation strategy at your company? Have you thought about how you can use social media to bring marketing by your community of friends into your customer and partner marketing campaigns today? Do you consider this strand of conversational marketing important at all? Are you looking at your competitors and watching how they are using online community tools to gain advantages over you? Do you currently have a two-way, push–pull marketing strategy or do you plan to promote your brand using the voice of the community talking about you and creating user generated content on your behalf?

THE NEW WAY OF MARKETING

By looking at best practices from leading companies and reviewing what others are doing today in their engagement with the community, you can start to create your strategic plan. You can integrate community marketing and your learning from online user behaviours to engage, share and drive conversations with customers and partners online. Using social engagement technologies, you can explore how to create demand and excitement for Web 2.0 interaction. You can create new marketing and selling opportunities and you can gain new insights into your audience.

> You can use conversational marketing to drive your own local marketing efforts to capture mindshare and increase satisfaction amongst your customers.

Perhaps the term 'social media' has skewed your perception about this new form of marketing. Underneath the glitz, the viral propagation and the news, is this really the way that you want to communicate with your customers? Do you already engage in some form of social communication? Are you communicating with your customers, partners, friends and competitors? Are you helping out your community, are you working with your virtual friends? Are your friends amplifying your message or are you collaborating with intent? And if you are collaborating with intent, what is the benefit to you? What is the value to your customers?

Every link we share, every blog we post, every video we upload adds to community collaboration and contributes to the conversation.

Comments, rebroadcasts, interaction and discussion add to brand awareness. The 'word of mouse', as Seth Godin terms this phenomenon, increases potential sales. An increase in sales leads to revenue growth and a better ROI for your digital marketing efforts. But before you launch your brand onto all of the engagement channels, you need to clearly define and develop your strategy and plan. You need a comprehensive plan and you need to define goals for what you want to achieve.

Once you have a strategy and an objective to achieve your goals, you need to think about how your brand will be perceived. In the next chapter we'll start to think about your online brand.

SUMMARY

- Classified social media sites are useful for B2C opportunities.
- Choose your site wisely. There are social networking sites for every purpose.
- Getting your campaign to go viral can be very good for business.
- Twitter can be used to broadcast and receive relevant news in almost real time.
- Generation Y uses social media sites in a different way than older users, and this should be taken into account when planning marketing campaigns.
- Conversational marketing increases mindshare and increases satisfaction.
- Does your strategy take into account push–pull marketing and conversational marketing? It should.

6   THE ONLINE BRAND

The first thing to consider about having a presence online is, quite simply, what you want people to think when they first meet you. By 'you' we might mean your product, your firm, or your cause, rather than you personally. The essence of that first impression is important as it is continued through repeated social online interaction. That essence is something you need to determine before showing your face at the party or getting your foot in the door.

Part of presenting your online brand is considering the medium and the tools you will use.

This is really critical because not all businesses should use all tools.

This chapter will show you what goes into distilling that essence into something that works for you as well as your customers. But how do you get the best out of the web?

Think about how you intend to promote your brand on the web and also how the 'personality of your brand (whether your brand represents a product or your own persona) works well in the social media world. It's no coincidence that the medium most often used to demonstrate the fun or quality of a new video game is video. Only through movement and monitoring actual game play can customers get a sense of what's in it for them when they purchase the new first-person shooter. If you are a better public speaker than writer, you may well consider having audio podcasts or video as your online medium of choice, because it will show your ideas and yourself in the best light. Likewise, if you are more a person of words than pictures, choosing a medium that relies more heavily on deftness with text (Twitter, blogging, Internet Relay Chat, etc.) may be the place to begin. The expense to the business has to be weighed against what the business wants to get done. Small businesses won't necessarily have the money to spare for big fancy video or sound production equipment.

As part of this discussion we will also look into what can go wrong when using the online tools. We will look at issues such as identity theft, reputation damage, profile-jacking, and harassment. While these may not deter you from an online presence, it's best to consider what can go wrong and to try to protect against these scenarios from the beginning. We will also consider what can be done when clones of you start to appear across the web. We will look at how you can measure your online brand effectiveness or reputation. Just as a partygoer may need a trusted friend to help her realise there is piece of spinach caught in her teeth, so do businesses and business people need measurable and objective targets to gauge how well they are doing online. We will cover some of the ways to determine if things have gone horribly wrong as well, if your brand or personal identity has been hijacked, or if the customers are not reacting as well to your brand as you'd hoped.

Finally, we will look at how brands can change over time. An online brand may be slower to change than its human makers –but brands can and do change, and figuring how to finesse an existing brand morphing into a new one is a good and potentially profitable exercise.

MANAGING YOUR BRAND

Managing your online brand is key to your success. It is important to make sure that the information you want to be released is on message, accurate and positive. And with this type of personal engagement offering the potential for things to go very wrong, it can be rather daunting.

> There is a lot of buzz around social media and social networking sites at the moment, and in order to keep your business at the forefront of your industry you need to be part of the conversation.

The move away from traditional push marketing to pull marketing and the word of mouth network is creating a more dynamic and engaging marketplace for your brand. If you are looking to buy a book on Amazon, you'll often look at the recommendations from others who have bought the book. You may also look at other recommended books to go with your original choice.

> Peer recommendations are powerful and can clinch deals.

Listening to your online and offline friends is much more powerful than buying from a static website. People buy from people, so an effective and positive brand is an important tool to have.

Good PR, bad PR

A great example of a company carefully managing its online brand is Apple. Everything that gets out into the 'open', so to speak, is carefully managed and controlled from a PR, messaging and brand perspective. This approach ensures that Apple's outbound messages are exactly what the company wishes to convey. This generates a huge amount of excitement among Apple fans desperate for news about future products. Forums, blogs and tweets abound speculating about the latest releases. The fans of Apple products create buzz and excitement from tiny snippets of the corporate message and no access at all to early versions of the products.

Compare that style of messaging with the approach taken by Microsoft. When Microsoft prepares to release a new version of its software, it releases very early beta copies of the code out to thousands of software and hardware testers. These testers have signed a Non-Disclosure Agreement, yet copies of this beta code sometimes find their way out onto peer to peer file sharing sites such as Bit Torrent. The early version of the code is discussed and speculated upon at length by the community and by technology journalists. If Microsoft subsequently decides to withdraw a component from the product build for whatever reason, or decides to fork, or create a new direction of the software build, perhaps deciding to drop certain features as they move forward with product development, then their brand and reputation can suffer in the press as a result.

These different approaches to product marketing seem to have very different results. Microsoft's apparent openness, which works really well with the concepts of social media marketing, often disappoints the audience. Apple, on the other hand, with its obsession with secrecy and lack of openness in social media spaces, generates an evangelical following by saying almost nothing.

So how do you manage your brand effectively? Brand management is all about making certain that you have a consistent message. It's about making sure that everyone inside the company follows your messaging guidelines and knows what to say. It's about damage control if there are problems further down the line. It's about consistency and communication. It's actually about empowering your employees and trusting them. And it's very hard to do that well without proper guidelines in place.

Your Twitter messages (tweets) can be seen by more people than you can imagine. James Andrews, who tweets under the name of @KeyInfluencer, was due to do a presentation in Memphis. James worked for Ketchum, a global PR management agency, and his presentation was intended for the Communications group at FedEx whose head office is in Memphis. He arrived at the airport in Memphis in January 2009 and sent a Twitter message (Figure 6.1) to his followers.

Figure 6.1 The tweet that upset a FedEx Employee

True confession but I'm in one of those towns where I scratch my head and say "I would die if I had to live here!

10:58 PM Jan 14th, 2009 from twhirl   ↶ Reply ⇄ Retweet

keyinfluencer
James Andrews

A FedEx employee saw the tweet and wrote an email. He copied his mail not only to the Ketchum directors and vice-presidents, but also up the management chain at FedEx. FedEx was founded in Memphis and is the city's largest private employer. The Employee Communications team responded to James:[19]

Many of my peers and I feel this is inappropriate. ... A hazard of social networking is people will read what you write.

Two days later, James posted a response on his website:[20]

Two days ago I made a comment on Twitter that was the emotional response to a run in I had with an intolerant individual. Everyone knows that at 140 characters Twitter does not allow for context and therefore my comments were misunderstood. If I offended the residents of Memphis, TN I'm sorry. That was not my intention.

Ketchum responded in a statement: *'It was a lapse in judgment and we've apologized to our client. We greatly value the longstanding relationship. It is our privilege to work with them.'*

Now there may be an underlying story other than the one splashed all over the blogosphere, and reading through the many comments after his post, there were speculations about other reasons. But I suppose it comes back to a simple tenet about publishing on the Internet:

Quite simply, don't publish anything online that you wouldn't want to be written on your headstone, or indeed, quoted back at you by a barrister in a court of law.

STARTING TO CREATE YOUR PERSONAL BRAND

I'm often dismayed at some of the photos I see on Facebook and other sites which have been uploaded by people who aren't in my immediate network of friends. These photos are visible to me through the fact that the photos of my friends have been tagged by **their** friends. Unfortunately some of these photos are inappropriate and not photos I'd want to see on the page of one of my team. I'm a manager and I look on various different networking sites like Facebook and LinkedIn to find out information about people who could be potential employees. I'm saddened to see the lack of thought and discretion by some people in my extended network. These people are not my direct acquaintances. They are the friends of my direct acquaintances, so they are one step out of my immediate network. People are also sometimes indiscreet on Twitter too. James Andrews's tweet could potentially have damaged a good customer relationship, which is certainly not the thing to do in these uncertain times. In the run-up to the 2010 general election in the UK, Stuart Maclennan was removed as a candidate from the Scottish Labour Party after 'totally unacceptable language which he has expressed online'

On Facebook, the profile settings allow you to display various pieces of information on your public profile. You can include your private email address on the public page. This does have its drawbacks, however. Sometimes when I've been researching potential employees, or business partners, I've been hesitant to take the conversation further due to some of the information I've found on the public profile.

If you're considering starting off and creating your own personal online brand or you wish to project a more positive image of yourself than might already be on the web, there are some basic steps you can take to get you started.

- Search for your name on the Internet. If someone has written something bad about you then it's likely that your prospective employer will have seen it. If you are searching for a job a recruitment agency will also find any information about you when they search for your details.

- Try to connect with all of your contacts online. Find the relevant addresses and make the connection with everyone in your network. Be careful, however, that harvesting contacts from your work contacts list might be in breach of your company privacy policy.

- Get a website – or, if you're hesitant about your coding skills, get a blog. You need to have a presence on the web. You may consider your website to be a static business card with your online curriculum vitae and details of your skills. If you have a blog and ensure that it is regularly updated, it will rise higher in search stack rankings and make your investment in time pay off in the long run.

- If you're publicising your email address to one and all, make sure that you have sensible email names. Names like studmuffin@mymail.com and evilbitch@yourmail.com may be funny when you're still at college, but you need to consider whether a prospective employer wants to hire you for that top job you've been looking for.

- Makes sure your LinkedIn, Facebook and Twitter profiles display appropriate information. You may think that the information that you've put into these is pithy, witty and humorous. Consider whether your next employer would think that your brand is appropriate.

- Contribute to the conversation. Don't spend your time lurking on sites that you find. If you have something interesting and relevant to say, add to the conversation and get your voice and ideas heard.

- If you do blog, remember to link, link, and link. Refer on your blog to quality posts you find, and acknowledge people that link to you. Links equate to reputation and credibility. Retweet interesting tweets and thank people who retweet your messages.

- Be careful what you say on your Twitter, Facebook and LinkedIn feeds. Do you really want to share too much information and go into detail about your personal life? Bleeping the swear words out with *** doesn't really help if you're trying to create the correct image online.

- Consider the friends of friends networks. I may not follow you on Twitter directly, but I may follow someone who follows you. How can you guarantee that people who contact you are not saying something in a conversation to you that will upset a prospective employer? Use the blocking feature of Twitter if you're concerned about someone's continued use of inappropriate messages.

- Create a business card with your email address, Skype name, Twitter name, LinkedIn profile, Facebook page and blog URL. Make your online brand addresses visible and make sure that you drive everyone to your online brand.

- If you use Facebook for your private and public personas, then learn to use the privacy settings within the application (Figure 6.2). Make sure that only the information that you want to publicise outside your network of accepted friends is actually the information you wish the world to see.

- Publicise your brand. Everywhere. The most successful online experts are everywhere you happen to look. They contribute and interact with their friends and colleagues on social networks, they comment on blogs and they are very vocal. They are also very well known across the web.

Figure 6.2 Where to apply Facebook privacy settings

I use the privacy settings on my profiles across the various websites I use regularly and layer different settings like an onion (Figure 6.3). As you get closer and closer to me and get to know me personally, you will find out more and more about me. Visiting my website gives you a limited amount of information about me, viewing my profile on Twitter gives you a little more. Finally I use my Facebook account for the most personal aspects of my personal life and my business life.

Corporate pages on Facebook
Investing in brand management takes time and effort. You will completely underestimate the investment in time required to make your digital brand successful. It's not at all easy to keep up an interesting, regular flow of articles,

Figure 6.3 My 'onion layer' approach to my privacy settings

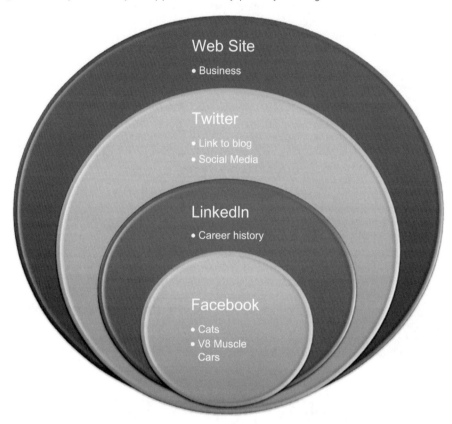

status updates and information for your audience. However, if you keep your messages topical, thought provoking, interesting or even controversial you'll see the conversation intensify and will start to reap the rewards.

Facebook has been used for personal friendships since its inception, but over time, with the increase in the number of users, companies have started to get involved. Companies have pages dedicated to promoting their business, and Facebook allows groups to be created, which fans can join, so that businesses can promote their special offers and encourage people to become fans. Facebook recognised the need to have corporate identities using unique names on the site. In May 2009 Facebook permitted personal user names for profiles and pages. Your Facebook profile or page for your business appears as

http://www.facebook.com/WorkingTheCrowd/

instead of

```
http://www.facebook.com/profile.php?id=123456789
```

Entering a Facebook username as a search term on Facebook or searching for that name on the web enables people to find friends and organisations with common names.

Companies, who own the right to their company name, sometimes find that their name has been pre-registered by cyber squatters. Fortunately they can make the business case to Facebook to have their name restored to them. Facebook states that it reserves 'the right to remove and/or reclaim any username at any time for any reason and that if someone's username infringes a company's intellectual property rights then there are ways to reclaim that name by filling in the IP infringement form'.[21] Hopefully you might still be able to claim your rightful company name on Facebook if you haven't done so already.

Pseudonyms and staying anonymous

There's a cartoon that's been doing the rounds on the Internet for years. The image is of a dog at a computer and the caption reads 'On the Internet, no one knows you're a dog'. It was created by Peter Steiner for the *New Yorker* magazine back in 1993. It's a classic cartoon of the Internet age, and it highlights just how easy it is to fool everyone online because it's so easy to send and receive messages in relative anonymity.

Many bloggers enjoy posting without revealing their identity, and indeed some bloggers turn their hobby into a successful and lucrative venture. An example of anonymous blogging hit the news at the end of 2009. 'Belle de Jour' was a pseudonym for a blogger who wrote about her activities in the sex trade. She used her earnings to finance her PhD studies. Her blog was noticed by the *Guardian* newspaper which gave her the 'blog of the year' award in 2003. Her extremely well written blog appeared to be tailored so completely to male sexual fantasies that many journalists speculated that she was actually a man.

Her candid and scurrilous blog was published as a book, *The Intimate Adventures of a London Call Girl.* This book was subsequently turned into a TV series in the UK, starring Billie Piper as Belle. In November 2009 Belle decided to disclose her identity to the broadsheet newspapers in the UK, as she believed that a former boyfriend was about to reveal her identity in the tabloid press. Surprisingly enough, Belle revealed herself as Dr Brooke Magnanti. Brooke is a student of informatics, epidemiology and forensic science who works at Bristol University's Centre for Nanoscience and Quantum Information. Revealing her identity totally smashed the misconception that she was male or that she had been forced into the sex trade for other reasons than she stated in her blog.

There are different schools of thought about whether it matters if your messages online are from you as a representative of the company, or if you are communicating under a pseudonym. There are some bloggers who hide their identity in order to be more candid about the company that they work for. An example of a hidden identity is the Microsoft blogger who uses the name 'Mini MSFT'. Mini has been blogging anonymously about the inner workings of Microsoft since 2004 and has a huge readership. He or she has a policy of total anonymity which encourages employees to have an open discussion about the company and its inner workings on his blog. He is credited with changing some of the company's internal processes around the end of year pay review process which has led to greater transparency throughout the organisation. The blog called Fake Steve Jobs was written by someone who hid his identity for over a year before being revealed as the journalist Daniel Lyons, a writer at *Newsweek*.

Whilst these kinds of anonymous postings on blogs didn't detract from the quality of information, or do much damage to the writers involved, there are much darker sides to consider. There is a fundamental requirement to protect children from the darker parts of the Internet, and the new applications, with sharing, collaboration and interaction, can be a potential minefield for keeping our children safe online. The media portrayals of danger give individuals a grossly inaccurate view of what is actually happening which is influencing companies to create fixes and offer new technologies that are often not fixing the real problem. It is important to understand how to help your children be safe.

We hear stories of Internet grooming, and read about the efforts of CEOP (Child Exploitation and Online Protection) to try and encourage children to report any specific activity. Paedophiles engaging in grooming activities try to trick children into meeting them. They often pose as teenagers and post messages, complete with spelling mistakes, poor grammar and abbreviated words, to impersonate the younger generation. Unfortunately there are often news items reporting about teenage girls who have been lured into meeting older men with whom they have struck up a friendship on Facebook or similar social networking sites.

There are laws and guidelines on marketing to children, with restrictions on junk food marketing and using children's programs for product placement. You need to be aware that your marketing activities across these social media tools may be seen by children and you should take this into account when constructing your messaging activities.

Using authenticity to build trust with your customers

When blogging for an enterprise or corporation it is also important to remember that you are using these sites on behalf of the company so there are rules, adopted by most large companies, which essentially boil down to being authentic and disclosing your true identity. The journalist posing as Fake Steve Jobs never purported to be the real Steve Jobs, but his information appeared to be accurate enough for readers to speculate. Mini MSFT definitely works for Microsoft and is rumoured to be fairly senior, judging from his conversations at executive level. The identity, although fake, gives a valuable look into the inner workings of a large company and the anonymous comments from real Microsoft employees give the blog authenticity, even though the blogger's true identity is not revealed.

When you blog on behalf of the company, you should fully disclose who you work for from the start. If you are using engagement tools to communicate on behalf of a client or business relationship you should disclose this relationship. It doesn't need to be a paragraph of legal jargon, just a simple like 'I work for xxx and the views on this blog are my own and not those of the company'. You should never use a false identity or pseudonym to hide your true identity. If you blog on behalf of a product, brand or for another business reason, then the identity itself should identify the company it represents.

One of the main issues with concealing your identity and operating under an alias is the brand itself.

Authenticity is key to building and developing trust with your audience, and operating under a pseudonym – especially if your true identity is exposed at a later stage – can often lead to disappointment and lack of trust. Lack of authenticity online alters perceptions of your brand offline.

There is a much deeper issue around online authenticity and authenticity in general. Without a deep level of integrity and honesty which has got to be ingrained in your corporate culture, achieving authenticity online is difficult. People can easily see through online activities that don't show authenticity or any degree of transparency. This can lead to loss of reputation and poor brand perception.

Things to consider to improve perception about your brand:

- Engage your audience little and often. Communicate regularly and avoid intense bursts of activity followed by deathly silences.
- Don't spam your audience with the same message over and over again. They will soon tire of the message.
- Social media works because it is a dialogue between members of the community. Listen to your audience. Engage them and interact with them.
- Don't disparage the competition. Your own company has its faults too.
- Be authentic. Show your audience the human side of your company.

It is so easy to add a new media channel for every campaign you launch and to focus your efforts entirely on achieving your reach metrics, interaction or engagement levels. But social networking is not a panacea for all digital marketing efforts. You will not improve poor brand perception with a short marketing campaign. Online execution is like adopting a healthy eating plan.

Only with diligence, dedication and long term adherence to the plan will you get the results you desire over time.

THE POTENTIAL FOR REPUTATION DAMAGE

Companies that have communities are well aware of the need to monitor and maintain the positive effects of the community, and that means instilling a sense of community health. Moderators use sophisticated tools to search for content that is considered inappropriate, or to watch for patterns of behaviour that could be deemed unsuitable. Bullying, impersonation to groom children for nefarious means, abuse, and child pornography need to be monitored very carefully, and stopping unsuitable behaviour is an urgent imperative. But in these task-rich, time-poor days how often do you look at your network to watch for these effects?

If you're using a system where friends of friends are free to post content you need to be very aware of what is happening outside your immediate network. For example, if someone is posting pornographic images on their own profile, what effect is this having on their friends? What are your friends doing? What are **their** friends doing? Issues like this then become more than an individual problem, they become a network problem. The US Air Force cancelled their online profile on MySpace due to precisely these concerns.[22] Col. Brian Madtes, chief of the Recruiting Service's strategic communication division, said:

The danger with MySpace is we got to the point where we weren't real comfortable with the potential for inappropriate content to be posted [on the page of] a friend of a friend. We didn't want to be associated with that ... and tarnish our reputation.

But everything isn't always as clear cut as it seems. If you chop off whole parts of the established network then the network will fragment and crumble. The health of the community has a great deal to do with the network. Using appropriate monitoring tools and judiciously blocking miscreants might be better in the long term than pruning whole segments of the environment. And it may have a much larger impact than you think. Google, which carries out continuous monitoring, took a bold stand in January 2010 when it stated that it was pulling out of China as it believed that sophisticated cyber attacks were being attempted on human rights activists in the country. However, consider the effect on the majority of the Chinese people who use the service. Prune your network wisely.

Vitriol, harassment and spite
There is also the issue of people with personal brands who are targeted by others, being bullied and terrorised. Kathy Sierra, considered to be one of technology's 'A list' bloggers, experienced this at first hand. Kathy, whose blog is called 'Creating Passionate Users', received death threats and harassment from unnamed persons. These threats and comments terrified her so much she stopped going to public events, stopped blogging and disappeared from the public eye for quite

some time. Fortunately, with her excellent personal and online brand and reputation, she received considerable support from the blogosphere which helped her return to online life.

Some people on the Internet create fake IDs, send out cruel backbiting messages and place comments on sites using these fake IDs. Such behaviour, which can turn vitriolic and nasty, is thinly disguised harassment delivered by cowards.

Preparing for negative PR

There are lessons to be learned here. It is hard to build a great reputation, and it can easily be destroyed. Nestlé, one of the food giants, has long been criticised over its poor environmental practices over deforestation and palm oil and its 'unethical use and promotion of formula feed for babies in third world countries'.[23] Nestlé has a Facebook page which became the target of many unhappy people advocating a boycott of the company over these practices. The administrators of the Facebook page took a hostile approach to the comments made on Twitter and Facebook and responded on Facebook accordingly.

With Facebook numbers currently at almost 600 million users, and the concept of friends telling friends, this PR disaster has amplified very quickly.

It no longer takes years to reach millions of users, it now takes minutes.

Nestlé representatives complained about some of the comments from Facebook users on their page. They initially deleted posts which were critical of the company and complained about use of Nestlé's altered logo. Unfortunately, the situation quickly appeared to get out of hand, with hundreds of negative comments appearing on Nestlé's Facebook page. This is not the first time that Nestlé has been in the news; Wikipedia has examples of previous issues concerning Nestlé. The interesting phenomenon here is that the use of social media has accelerated the runaway propagation of information into almost meltdown proportions. This is something that may do damage to Nestlé's reputation entirely due to their initial attitude towards their Facebook fans.

I heard an interesting story at an event I attended recently about a social media site which has become notorious in a very short time and has got its social media PR entirely wrong. The site is called Fit Finder and it has the tagline 'Witness the Fitness'. This site isn't very politically correct but it has a huge following. Fit Finder has a feed for each college or university where you can post information anonymously on where the good-looking students are. All you do is fill in a form so that anyone subscribing to the feed can see where they are right now.

As I said, the site isn't politically correct, and one of the universities had a couple of complaints about harassment. The college, which has a policy of not blocking sites, then sent out an email telling everyone not to visit the site. Traffic to the site rocketed, which led to more complaints about the content on the site.

JANET (the Joint Academic NETwork in the UK) then blocked access to the site. This meant that all universities, schools and colleges had no access from their PCs. However, anyone with a mobile device or other wireless connection could access the site and log on to see what the fuss was about. Another major spike in traffic happened and awareness of the site grew. The *Guardian* and the London *Metro* covered the story, with *Metro* further reporting about the start of the mobile revolution occurring. The Facebook page grew to over 4,000 fans and the feed at all college locations is updated regularly.

JANET, after multiple complaints from universities around the UK, unblocked access to the site again. There are regular updates – lots of them seem to be by girls commenting on boys, so there do seem to be roughly equal numbers of comments for both males and females on the site.

There are a couple of lessons that can be learned about managing social media PR:

- Don't tell people not to visit a site, as it's the first thing that they will want to do – especially if the site seems scurrilous or controversial.

- A blanket blocking by an organisation such as JANET will drive people to visit the site using other means. Mobile device updates, Facebook updates and Twitter notifications keep awareness right up there.

If no one had said anything, traffic to the site might have fizzled out in a few weeks or months. Instead, its notoriety has ensured its continued success. Fit Finder follows a similar model to Facebook, which is now 7 years old and hugely different now than when it started. I wonder if Fit Finder will have the same sort of success. It seems to have started off rather well.

A simple YouTube video can also trigger a similar propagation explosion. In early 2008 Dave Carroll, a musician in a band, flew with his guitar from Nova Scotia to Nebraska via Chicago on United Airlines. One of his band mates saw the baggage handlers heaving around the guitars with 'wanton disregard'. Dave complained to the flight attendants but his comments were met with indifference. When he arrived at his destination to play at the event he found his guitar was broken. He played at his gig, and complained to the airline upon his return and for several weeks afterwards. He spent $1,200 repairing the guitar and claimed compensation from the airline. Unfortunately this claim was denied by the airline because he didn't complain 'in the right place or at the right time'. Dave told United Airlines that he was going to write a song and post it on YouTube, but the company ignored his threat.

The 'United breaks guitars' video went viral very quickly, and soon had over 8 million views on YouTube.[24] This online video managed to connect with the airline. United Airlines responded to the video and 'put things right' for him. By eventually responding to the issue and fixing their customers' issues, United showed that they could reverse the impressions created by their original poor service.

Tackling customers' problems in a timely and positive manner can bring significant benefits to the company. After investing your efforts to create a positive online brand, this is certainly something worth considering as your brand grows in prominence.

So you now have a brand and a presence on the web. People already have a perception of your brand, so now let's have a look at how to make the brand more successful. With success come challenges, and we'll consider what to do so as to stay within your guidelines. What guidelines? Let's now have a look at how to create a framework for your staff to work with.

SUMMARY

- You need to be part of the conversation.
- Don't underestimate the power of peer recommendations.
- Consider your current approach to marketing. Will it still work in the social media world?
- People will read what you write. There is no delete key.
- Consider your privacy settings in each application and review them regularly.
- Consider creating a page in Facebook for business.
- Manage your reputation carefully and take prompt action to rectify any damage to your brand.
- Be aware of the impact on your brand reputation and image if there are issues.

7   BRAND IMPACT AND BRAND SUCCESS

In this chapter we'll start to look at what makes your brand successful amongst your audience. We'll look at how customers want to feel about your brand and your engagement with them. We'll talk about how companies like Dell have used this to their advantage and obtained measurable financial results. We'll also look at how companies adopt policies and guidelines for their staff. We'll look at good and not so good examples of policies and innovative ways of getting the message out. We'll talk about legal aspects and consider some potential issues around intellectual property and copyright. Finally, we'll look at established brands and how they tackle brand migration. Some have managed this brand shift very successfully, others less so. We'll have a look at some things to consider in the digital world if you feel that you want to do the same.

THE IMPACT OF SOCIAL MEDIA INSIDE YOUR BUSINESS

You know what your business is all about. You have defined objectives and metrics that you measure. You have specific actions that you refine regularly and you're ready to add social media marketing to your digital marketing strategy. Unfortunately, this is often where things start to go wrong.

> This flood of communication and interaction has been building for more than 25 years and it is fundamentally changing the way that businesses and customers interact.

It is as vital to business success as was mass production in the industrial revolution, the impact of the PC and the growth of the web.

> This interaction is very important for you, your business and your customers.

Why are networks so important to you and your business? Social media impacts your sales, gives a great insight into market intelligence, and gathers information directly from your customers. It can refine your logistics, contribute to your research and refine your product development cycle. It is crucial to your success in business. You may pay for market analysis, look at your click-through figures to find out unique visitors to your pages and where they are from, but that's about it. How can you find out how these users are grouped? Is there a network cluster that you can define? Is there a social graph connecting your users? Is it strong and growing? Or is it fragmented and weak? Where are the strong and weak ties in your network? How do you know who your influencers are?

When you're deciding to introduce these conversational tools into your traditional marketing approach, you know that you want to get your marketing message out to your customers. Unfortunately, some companies tend to use all of the channels that they know. This sometimes comes across like a message distributed by scatter gun to the audience. The 'launch' of a blog, the fanfare over the creation of a Facebook page, a new Twitter name, a Friendfeed list or a YouTube channel are all great ideas which will prove valuable to you if you've identified the appropriate channel for your message.

> Many companies forget what type of messages they are trying to broadcast to their customers and the response they are trying to achieve – the message comes before the medium.

Knowing your customer

When preparing to complement your marketing activities with your social media plan, consider what motivates your customers' behaviour online. This means that you need to think about separating your customers into different groups according to their behaviour. And that means looking at their age.

GROUPING CUSTOMERS

- If you're targeting customers who are aged between the ages of 20 and 30, think about competitions. This age group tends to be competitive. They set themselves ambitious targets and compete with their peers.

- Between the ages of 30 and 40, customers like to have an understanding and awareness of who they are and where they fit into the larger model. Perhaps they have defined themselves as working class or middle class. If they know how important they are to your brand they can understand why you are communicating with them and how they can help.

- Customers aged between 45 and 60 tend to seek affirmation that the decisions that they have made are the correct one, so brand value plays a large role in their decision making process.

Essentially, the consumer wants you to acknowledge that they are valued.

> It's all about me – understand me, acknowledge me, and know who I am and what I represent.

Once a brand has done this, then your business is well on the way to persuading them to become advocates and enthusiasts. You also need to remember that your business mind is quite different from your customer's mind. For you it's about revenue, profit, power, growth, status, work, money and sex, whereas customers will be thinking about family, home, F1, football, celebrities, kittens, money and sex. Since the dotcom boom, consumers have moved towards a more web-centric method of purchasing and interacting. The web is now widely used for shopping, and with social tools displaying birthdays and status updates people are much more willing to share more personal details about themselves online. This new attitude contrasts completely with our face to face lives, when only our closest friends get to share the personal details of our life such as our birth date, relationship details and hobbies.

USING TWITTER TO GROW YOUR BUSINESS – DELL STYLE

Dell is a great example of an organisation that has benefited from using the new communication tools. It had very a specific and targeted business purpose, which was to increase sales revenues and decrease support costs. It decided to spread its methods of communicating with its customers across several channels. Dell has blogs, four Twitter accounts, several Facebook pages and a YouTube channel. Dell features time-limited 'special offers' in its Twitter feeds; its YouTube channel has over 500 videos. These videos showcase new products, feature discussions with product managers showing innovation in products, and display the results of student competitions. In this case, Dell knows how the under 30s feel the need to compete with each other. Dell's blogs are full of useful information from the product team, but there is also a wealth of information from people who have knowledge of the product set.

DELL'S COMMUNITY SUCCESS

Dell's community is contributing to the expansion of knowledge by effective peer to peer support. This support is lowering the cost of each support call to Dell. The answers to customers' questions can often be found on the forums, written by another member of the community.

This approach has brought Dell measurable results. Figure 7.1 shows the number of people following the Dell Outlet Twitter account from March to June 2009. On 7 March it had around 117,000 followers, on 7 June there were almost 609,000; by 1 January 2010 the number exceeded 1.5 million.

These followers are looking for Dell offers that are exclusively announced on Twitter.

These offers are retweeted by many of the Dell Outlet Twitter followers, which creates buzz for Dell and has helped to grow Dell's follower base.

According to Stephanie Nelson, who started tweeting as the @DellOutlet account, deal hunters are especially attracted to Dell's Twitter presence.[25] Dell Outlet sells

Figure 7.1 @Dell Outlet Twitter follower growth March to June 2009

(Source: TwitterCounter.com)

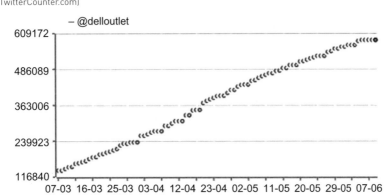

refurbished Dell products at great prices, but inventories fluctuate, making it difficult to know when products are available or on sale. Dell Outlet uses Twitter as a way to message out coupons, clearance events and new arrival information to those looking for Dell technology at a discounted price.

This innovation has generated Dell over $3 million in revenue (to the end of 2009), and as a global brand, Dell has recognised the need to duplicate this success in other countries.[26] Now Dell has other accounts: @DellOutletUK, @DellOutletIE, @DellHomeSalesAU and @Offertas_Dell_MX, to name a few. Dell has even linked its Twitter activity to a web page on its site to round the experience out for the consumer, which seems to have done a great deal for its brand image too.

CORPORATE GUIDELINES AND POLICIES

Companies are starting to regard social networking sites, forums and message boards as significant to the business. These forums contain important content, and companies recognise that they need to apply policies that govern the acceptable use of this content. But is it possible to define an acceptable standard for user generated content? Do you apply something that prohibits the use of social engagement tools in any form whilst inside the corporate firewall? Some companies prohibit blogging, or they block Facebook and Twitter through the corporate firewall. Some companies issue such severely restrictive policies that they are almost impossible to comply with.

ESPN, the sports news channel, has issued very specific and detailed guidelines for social networking for any of their staff engaged with the public discussing sports news:[27]

- Personal websites and blogs that contain sports content are not permitted.
- Prior to engaging in any form of social networking dealing with sports, you must receive permission from the supervisor as appointed by your department head.

- ESPN.COM may choose to post sports related social media content.

- If ESPN.com opts not to post sports related social media content created by ESPN talent, you are not permitted to report, speculate, discuss or give any opinions on sports related topics or personalities on your personal platforms.

- The first and only priority is to serve ESPN sanctioned efforts, including sports news, information and content.

- Assume at all times you are representing ESPN.

- If you wouldn't say it on the air or write it in your column, don't tweet it.

- Exercise discretion, thoughtfulness and respect for your colleagues, business associates and our fans.

- Avoid discussing internal policies or detailing how a story or feature was reported, written, edited or produced and discussing stories or features in progress, those that haven't been posted or produced, interviews you've conducted, or any future coverage plans.

- Steer clear of engaging in dialogue that defends your work against those who challenge it and do not engage in media criticism or disparage colleagues or competitors.

- Be mindful that all posted content is subject to review in accordance with ESPN's employee policies and editorial guidelines.

- Confidential or proprietary company information or similar information of third parties who have shared such information with ESPN, should not be shared.

Any violation of these guidelines could result in a range of consequences, including but not limited to suspension or dismissal.

These steps are logical and considered, but perhaps a little too restrictive for employees. Some of the bullet points seem to oversimplify certain details. A lot of these guidelines could form part of the standard employee guidelines and be set out in an employee handbook, and reference made to this from the company's social media policy.

In the 1920s the United States applied prohibition to alcohol, which immediately led to hundreds of illicit outlets springing up and operating illegally. There are indications that this level of restriction may foster similar behaviour online. Users will start to use their personal mobile devices to engage in digital conversations whilst at work.

Telstra, the Australian telecommunications and media company, had an innovative way to announce its social guidelines for its staff. It published its training guide on the web in an easy to read comic book format. This guide has links to videos, two of which have been published on YouTube. This is a great way to make sure everyone inside and outside the company sees the guidelines that Telstra has published, and knows how they work. They're simple and straight forward too. Publishing in this way, online for everyone to see and search for on the web, is a great initiative. Telstra certainly appears to be leading the way here, and should be applauded for its efforts. The new form of engagement is all about discoverability, communication and channelling the torrent of information into something manageable, constructive and useful.

So what would a good corporate social media policy contain? Here are some core principles that I believe are a good foundation for policy guidelines:

GENERAL SOCIAL MEDIA POLICY GUIDELINES

- Be respectful of others. Don't insult, disparage, libel, defame, inflame or attack others.
- Be true to yourself. Authenticity and integrity must underpin all of your communications.
- Be accurate. Fake social media campaigns are soon exposed and credibility is soon lost.
- Be respectful of corporate intellectual property. Protect copyright or confidential corporate information.
- Bring value to your readers. They are potential future clients and connections and their satisfaction matters.
- Be humble. You cannot be right all of the time. Acknowledge your errors and apologise with humility.
- Be generous. Acknowledge other authors where you've used their work.
- Be responsible. You are the company spokesperson in your external messaging.
- Be thoughtful. An off the cuff comment can do immense damage to your reputation and corporate brand.
- Be careful. Think before you post.
- Do not speculate on matters that may prejudice your company in any legal case.

Another good tip when you're writing your social media policy is to be concise. A good social media policy needs to be less than one page so that the contents are remembered. Keeping it simple is a great idea. IBM[28] has a simple, easy to read blogging policy and social media policy, as does Intel,[29] including these tips for engaging in global conversations:

- Stick to your area of expertise and provide unique, individual perspectives on what's going on at Intel and in the world.
- Post meaningful, respectful comments—in other words, no spam and no remarks that are off-topic or offensive.

Intel's rules of engagement follow similar themes to other companies which have published their guidelines on the web and can be summarised as follows:

- Respect brands, copyrights and trademarks.
- Add value to your customers and readers. Build a sense of community.
- If it gives you pause, pause. If you're about to publish something that makes you even the slightest bit uncomfortable, don't shrug it off and hit 'send'.

Twitter guidelines

With the rise of Twitter for customer interaction, there are other specific policies that could be applied to microblogging. If you're using Twitter as a way to communicate with your customers and provide great customer service from the brand, you might want to modify your style somewhat.

GUIDELINES FOR USING TWITTER

- If you get customer questions, respond quickly to keep the dialogue flowing.
- Ask questions of your audience – don't just broadcast.
- Do not be derogatory about your competitors.
- Twitter should not be the only tool used for customer maintenance. All requests need to be redirected back to the appropriate support team for action and recording.
- Respect corporate legal guidelines, and confidentiality.
- If you're using a specific Twitter name, like SubaruSupport, make sure that your messages are relevant to your brand.
- If you have a corporate account, keep to corporate messages and don't flood the stream with information about your personal life.
- Tweet about what you know – stick to your area of expertise.
- Make sure your messages are interesting or compelling or newsworthy.
- Make sure that you are committed to maintaining your Twitter presence. Co-opt others into helping you populate the Twitter stream.
- Be careful who you follow, and don't automatically follow everyone who follows you. Watch out for automated bots, and aim for quality not quantity.
- Use hashtags to talk about themes so you can search for tweets using these themes to track your metrics. Try to keep these hashtags short. You only have 140 characters, so #followfriday has, over time, been shortened to #ff to save space.
- Retweet other interesting tweets.
- Use short URLs like http://bit.ly which have metrics showing click-through totals.

If you have a clearly defined social media policy and blogging policy and you have raised awareness amongst your staff and everyone follows the rules, then you don't really need to not worry. Over time, you will find that internal conversations occur within your organisation, the users will self-police their behaviour, and brand advocates will ensure that your brand message stays consistent. However, you need to consider things that may go wrong.

Keeping things legal

Who are you on the web? What do people know about you? If you search for your brand you will find mentions of it, but there may be items on the web that you might never have known were there. On a personal level, these facts may be innocuous, like your daughter talking about you and the job you do on her Facebook page or Twitter feed. It may be others in your network tweeting about your holiday antics in Spain last summer, your rugby skills, or a photograph of you downing that last vodka shot in a club. These exchanges are out there on the web, and you can't do anything about them – because you don't actually own them. They are out of your control and they have the potential to do your reputation great harm. In addition to effective corporate policies and basic common sense over what you broadcast on the Internet, a question arises about where the legal boundaries lie.

During the snowfall in February 2009 a blogger in the UK, Ben Marsh, created a mashup application on the web. He used a Google map and overlaid the map with Twitter hashtags showing where all of the snow was falling in the UK. He also displayed the tweets marked with the hashtag #uksnow as they appeared on Twitter from users around the UK. The hashtag #uksnow was widely adopted and reported in the media. Rory Cellan-Jones from the BBC received a message from a reader, Julian Bray, who said that he had 'invented' the hashtag and claimed it as his intellectual property.[30] This seemed to be the first time anyone had claimed intellectual property rights over a hashtag – after all, it's only a word. The http://hashtags.org website documents millions of hashtags in popular use on Twitter, and it's almost impossible to claim ownership of a word. The ability to do this could raise some interesting battles.

Twitter and copyright

If someone plagiarises content from a book and republishes it elsewhere, then the author has due recourse to the law of the land. If a piece of music is copied, cloned or reproduced, and the owner of the original piece of music can prove that the music has been plagiarised, then they also have a legal advantage in court. Trademarks are enforceable by law and counterfeit art is illegal. But what is the legal case if you repeat information that you found on Twitter or Facebook? Do you actually have any rights at all to the information you broadcast?

According to Twitter, what you write is yours.[31] Twitter copyright policy states:

Twitter respects the intellectual property rights of others and expects users of the Services to do the same. We will respond to notices of alleged copyright infringement that comply with applicable law and are properly provided to us. If you believe that your Content has been copied in a way that constitutes copyright infringement, please provide us with the following information:

(i)   a physical or electronic signature of the copyright owner or a person authorized to act on their behalf;

(ii) identification of the copyrighted work claimed to have been infringed;

(iii) identification of the material that is claimed to be infringing or to be the subject of infringing activity and that is to be removed or access to which is to be disabled, and information reasonably sufficient to permit us to locate the material;

(iv) your contact information, including your address, telephone number, and an email address;

(v)   a statement by you that you have a good faith belief that use of the material in the manner complained of is not authorized by the copyright owner, its agent, or the law; and

(vi) a statement that the information in the notification is accurate, and, under penalty of perjury, that you are authorized to act on behalf of the copyright owner.

Facebook has multiple approaches to copyright information, but their main policy says:[32]

We respect the intellectual property rights of others and we prohibit users from posting content that violates another party's intellectual property rights. When we receive a proper claim of IP infringement, we promptly remove or disable access to the allegedly infringing content. We also terminate the accounts of repeat infringers in appropriate circumstances.

So does this mean that if you retweet or share a comment on Twitter or Facebook, you are breaking copyright law? Theoretically, yes. However, tweets and comments are attributed to the owner of the tweet, typically via a retweet. Comments are attributed to the originator so that credit is given for their original quote. The United States Copyright Office Circular 34 states that copyright law does not protect names, titles, or short phrases or expressions.[33] Twitter is limited to 140 characters and theoretically a 'short phrase' as opposed to a long paragraph of text from a publication or online article.

But who actually owns these tweets? Twitter and Facebook both say that it is the originator of the message who owns them. Of course, if you were so obsessed about copyright, then perhaps you wouldn't broadcast your intellectual property on such a public site in the first place. Unless, of course, you want to have your information broadcast by your friends and your message amplified.

There might be someone on the web who may take issue with something you write.

Who owns your content?

Facebook changed its terms and conditions to reflect their stance about ownership of content:[34]

> You hereby grant Facebook an irrevocable, perpetual, non-exclusive, transferable, fully paid, worldwide license...to (a) use, copy, publish, stream, store, retain, ...reformat, modify, edit,... and distribute..., any User Content you (i) Post ... or (ii) enable a user to Post, ... and (b) to use your name, likeness and image for any purpose, ...

The important bit is this:

> You may remove your User Content from the Site at any time. If you choose to remove your User Content, the license granted above will automatically expire, however you acknowledge that the Company may retain archived copies of your User Content.

Several blogs picked this up from Facebook and an outcry ensued. Facebook reverted to its old terms within a few days. But what does this mean? Well, hopefully those photos of you downing vodka shots at the rugby reunion were taken by friends who have protected their Facebook profiles with appropriate privacy settings. Any photos which were not taken by you but have been tagged with your name and placed on other, unprotected profiles can be seen by anyone who searches for your name. Privacy settings are very important (and Facebook gives you the chance to untag any photos that you don't wish to broadcast further). Once you have set your privacy it is a good idea to regularly check your settings. Make sure that your specific settings are still valid as this will stop any problems if Facebook changes anything in the application which could potentially open up your data and photos to a wider group of connections.

If you have not spent some time setting your privacy settings correctly, think about this. In 20 years' time, when you're in a respectable position at work or you are thinking about becoming a councillor or a politician, remember that those Facebook photos can be accessed by anyone. Without the proper settings in place, they could come back to haunt you and your reputation.

It's certainly worth a thought. Vodka shot, anyone?

MANAGING REBRANDS AND BRAND MIGRATION

Things change at the speed of a mouse click nowadays. Change is inevitable in the Web 2.0 world. So how do you manage your brand status whilst preparing for a rebrand? There are right and wrong ways to go about the migration of your brand which will be largely determined by how much you want your customers to be influenced by your new brand and how much you want to change customer perception.

Have you considered the reasons for your rebrand? Mergers and acquisitions are often a great opportunity for a brand revamp. Symantec acquired Quarterdeck in November 1998 and renamed its product CleanSweep to Norton CleanSweep. Symantec subsequently repositioned the entire product line by bundling a suite of products together and naming it Norton SystemWorks. Other reasons to rebrand could be due to a decline in product perception amongst consumers. The rebranding of the Philip Morris brand to Altria was done to help the company shed its negative image when a court in the US ordered Philip Morris to pay $3 billion in damages to a smoker suffering terminal cancer who claimed he wasn't warned of the dangers of smoking.[35]

Things can go wrong with the product rebrand if it's not carried out to customer satisfaction. The UK Post Office's attempt to rebrand itself as Consignia proved to be such a failure that millions more had to be spent rebranding again to become Royal Mail. The branding of New Coke lasted 77 days before Coca-Cola switched the drink back to its original formula and renamed it Coke Classic.[36] People seemed to be more upset about the withdrawal of the old formula than the taste of the new one. The psychiatrist hired by Coca-Cola to listen in on phone calls to the company hotline told executives that some people sounded as if they were discussing the death of a family member. Pepsi has changed many of their brands. It recently renamed Mountain Dew as Mtn Dew and it has adjusted the Pepsi logo slightly. The red and blue areas within the circle have been modified to represent a series of 'smiles' on each of their product range.[37] Will it be successful? Only time and consumer conversation will tell.

A rebrand can be a great opportunity for you to take a long hard look at how your product is perceived in the digital world. Your traditional approach to your product sales on the Internet may be in the form of bricks and clicks marketing, integrating both an offline (bricks) and an online (clicks) presence. You order the product online, but you go to collect your product in person at the store. Any attempt at rebranding or brand migration needs to be effectively handled. Customers need to be made aware of the new plans through external marketing, and internal staff need training so that they can also talk about the new product or brand. A good design agency needs to be engaged early on in the process so that tight co-ordination can keep everyone on message throughout the process. Successful rebranding projects can yield a brand which is better regarded than it was before. The new company identity and brand could also be launched in a methodical manner to avoid alienating your existing customers, while aiming to attract new business prospects. Microsoft successfully achieved this with its search engine, Bing, which was an evolutionary step forward for their Live Search product and relaunched at the end of May 2009.

Controlling these marketing messages does seem to work. Figure 7.2 shows that when Bing was launched, searches performed on Google dipped for each spike in Bing.[38] Each of these spikes equates to an announcement about Bing – for example, the announcement that Bing was going to add Twitter real-time data to search results as well as indexing static Twitter profiles.[39]

If you're planning a similar brand migration, how do you migrate your brand to take advantage of the digital market?

Figure 7.2 Top search engines in the US from May to December 2009

MIGRATING YOUR BRAND

- This is a business move. Take the emotion out of the decision and try to be objective about it. An external agency can bring a fresh approach – without the emotion that you will have invested. The family firm that has been in business for years probably hasn't moved its brand strategy forward for a while.

- Companies usually start small and expand, sometimes exponentially, without a formal brand strategy in place. Make sure you have a strategy in place before embarking on a rebrand.

- Your brand is already successful. It's time to analyse which parts of it will work in the digital age. Is it the name, the image, the logo, the tag line, or even the colour? Make sure you keep the parts of the brand that are important to you.

- It doesn't have to be a major change. Think of the success that rebranding the term 'gambling' to 'gaming' has brought for the industry.

- Smaller companies find that there is lots of room for a major rebrand, while large companies, such as the Post Office, Hewlett-Packard and Microsoft, have to make sure that they avoid upsetting their existing customers. A rule of thumb is: the smaller the company, the larger the opportunity to rebrand, which is a great opportunity for entrepreneurs.

The mighty Disney Corporation, which has Mickey Mouse as one of its best known assets, is considering rebranding this iconic figure. Disney has created a new Mickey Mouse for a video game. Epic Mickey[40] has new cunning personality traits which he exhibits as he traverses the game. This brand migration of their most beloved character is risky, to say the least. But if Disney can pull this brand migration off with Mickey Mouse, then anyone can.

You now have a brand, a presence and guidelines to work with. What next? The next chapter gets you connecting and growing your network.

SUMMARY

- Social interaction is fundamentally changing the way we do business.
- Correctly classify and understand your customers and the way they behave online.
- Consider using Dell's approach to get business through Twitter.
- Create effective social media guidelines for your staff and educate them on your digital policy.
- Be aware of copyright and legal issues around repeating content.
- Consider the effects of rebranding and take steps to manage it properly.

8   CONNECTIONS AND REPUTATION

Connecting to others in the social networking space is simple. With social distance decreasing, and the friends of friends networks becoming closer, it seems easy to reach potentially anyone across the connected world. In this chapter we will look at how the web has morphed into a socially connected environment where users' behaviour has evolved over time and has grown to incorporate all ages, tastes and styles.

Discoverability is key to your success with social networking.

We'll consider ways to manage your reputation and how recommendations are vital to build a community and discover your influencers. We'll talk about the apparent differences in the way news propagates and how different types of networking applications cater to these styles. We'll also see how easy it is to monitor sentiment for your brand and to gauge your reputation. We'll work out some ways to mitigate brand-jacking and think about how to build your reputation if the worst does happen. Finally, we'll discuss the dangers that can occur if your identity is cloned and we'll look at some best practice ideas around managing passwords across different websites that you visit on the web.

MAKING SENSE OF SOCIAL NETWORKING

Do you have friends on Facebook, or do you prefer to connect on LinkedIn? Are you a tweeter, a lurker or a Plurker? Do you live in the world of instant news, video uploads, or do you constantly watch your status updates? Is your avatar a taller, thinner, better-looking and more exciting version of you? Do you live in your Second Life because it's more exciting than your first life? Do you aggregate your RSS feeds for viewing online in Google Reader, or offline with Sharpreader or Outlook? What is your favourite news feed service? How compact is your social graph? Where are you on Technorati? Meebo? IceRocket? What's your favourite wiki?

The web has morphed into something that lends itself perfectly to interaction, both synchronous and asynchronous.

The term 'Web 2.0' was first coined by Darcy DiNucci in 1999.[41] She predicted that the browser experience which delivered web content in 'static screenfuls' was 'only an embryo of the Web to come'. She said that the web would be used as the 'transport mechanism, the ether through which interactivity happens'. Her comments, now more than 11 years old, were far ahead of their time and are so true today.

The term 'Web 2.0' disappeared from general use but reappeared in 2003. Web 2.0 is now generally associated with Tim O'Reilly, who discussed the term at the Web 2.0 Conference in San Francisco. Even in 2003, Tim recognised that interaction between users was a significant business benefit. He brought industry leaders from companies like Amazon and Yahoo! to the conference to deliver their predictions. They talked about the emergence of the web as a platform which would deliver the applications, and the browser to deliver the application experience for the users.

Now the phrase of the moment seems to be 'social media'. Social media is actually an evolution of the term 'social software'. It's usually used in technical circles and is also known in academia as 'groupwork'. Social media is the latest in a long line of buzzwords. It is used to describe the collection of software, tools and services that brings users together into a massively collaborative environment. Here they can share, inform, gather, play, co-ordinate and communicate. These collaborators create user generated content which is used for the greater good of others. Wikipedia is a great example of the community freely giving their time and expertise to contribute to a document entirely to benefit others.

To delve into this evolutionary shift, we need to consider three factors:

SOCIAL NETWORKING EVOLUTION

- Social networking originally appeared to be attractive to the younger age groups and niche technologists. This has now changed, with all age groups from all walks of life engaging in social connection activities.

- Social networking sites have achieved a tremendous groundswell of followers. This network effect has rippled around the world gaining significant traction in many social circles, demographics and societies.

- With all groundswell effects we need to consider where they are going and what will be next in this behavioural interaction.

To understand how social networking works, we need to try to work out which aspects of social networking activities actually glue these communities together. There are certain behaviours that are important to the structure of engagement and interaction.

SOCIAL NETWORKING BEHAVIOURS

- Discoverability. With the sophistication of search, it's now fairly easy to find someone who has been posting content online. Historical content is saved and stored somewhere on cache servers. Search exposes us to a far wider spread of information due to these mechanisms. Unfortunately, this information can be used for bad activities as well as good.

- Location. With the rise in location based applications, you can add location and presence to your digital communications. Think about geocaching applications for example. With geocaching, objects and clues are hidden at specified places and discovered using geographic coordinates. With location aware services on mobile devices, we now have the opportunity to take a photograph, or a video, upload and share it immediately on social networking sites. If you add tagging to this functionality or recommendations from others, you can discover who else has been in the same location, when they were there, and what they thought of it. This functionality helps you to connect virtually with the community from your current physical location. This virtual location can now take you to any location across the world.

- Propagation. People forward on emails, cut and paste text from useful snippets and forward them on. Whether this is in the form of a status update, a retweet or a re-shared link, the value to others is the propagation of this information. Unfortunately, the ability to modify the original text to suit your opinions has the potential to replicate false information across the Internet.

- Recommendation. This is a double edged sword in social applications. Receiving recommendations can improve your profile, lead to referrals from your extended network and be of mutual benefit to both parties. However there are times when this interaction can also cause problems. Malicious rumours, negative comments, and ill chosen words can propagate around the Internet, doing significant damage to a reputation in a matter of hours. This propagation of information, once it is out there, is permanent.

- Connection. If I know someone whom I think you would benefit from meeting then I can connect you both together. This connection extends your network and can amplify any message you want to broadcast. You can decide whether you want to make the connection, for mutual benefit or business reasons. You can also decide not to proceed.

- Reputation. This is of enormous value to the user. If someone recommends you, a link you've shared, or likes your online status, your reputation increases in the eyes of your peers. MMORPGs have recognised this status and award badges, medals and tier points for obtaining arbitrary goals in the game. Reputation in gaming is similar to the value to the seller having an unblemished 100% feedback score on eBay, and it is visible across most online games.

Having the correct mechanisms in place to make effective connections is important. However, you also need knowledge about how communities interact, participate and lead the conversation. With this as a foundation, you can start to think about your social media architecture. You will then be able to formulate what your approach might be and how to create your strategic plan.

The digitally connected world

Much has been made of the term 'six degrees of separation'[42] to explain how connected the world is. The term actually originated in a book of short stories written by the Hungarian author Frigyes Karinthy.[43] The book talked about 'friendship networks' which could traverse great distances. Despite being physically separated by distance, the shrinking world and the increase in human population density make this 'social distance' appear much smaller than it has been in the past. The hypothesis about the six degrees of separation came about as a result of an experiment which speculated that any two people could be connected to each other by at most five connections. This concept actually influenced the early thinking about social networks.

Further experiments were conducted later by Stanley Millgram. Millgram tried to calculate the average path or hop length of a social network. He wanted to count the number of ties between any two people who passed a packet of information from Omaha and Wichita to Boston in the United States. People in these regions were randomly selected and sent packages explaining the purpose of the study. They were asked to send the package on to their known connections. There was a list on the package for the recipients to record their name and which part of the link they participated in.

Recipients of the package were asked to forward it on to someone they knew who might know the end recipient in the chain at Boston. If the end recipient was known, then the package went straight to them. Often the letters would arrive at the intended target in one or two hops; others would arrive at their target after more than nine links. The average number of hops to the destination seemed to be about 5.5.

An interesting facet of human behaviour appeared during this study which explains some people's behaviour on social networking sites. In some of these studies, the packages never arrived at their intended destination at all. Some of the recipients refused to forward the packages, bringing the chain to an end. In some tests, around 80% of packages were not forwarded on to their intended destination. In other cases, 66% of the letters were handed to the destination recipient by the same person. This person, a 'Mr Jacobs', whose occupation had something to do with clothing, must have had significant connections or ties to several of the other networks in the chain, making him a great connector. Malcolm Gladwell, the author of *The Tipping Point*, speculated that connectors are 'people specialists'. They know and like a lot of people, they collect acquaintances and they remember people in their network. Mr Jacobs must have been a great connector in his own network to receive so many packages to deliver on to his other networks.

COMMUNITY CONNECTIONS AND RECOMMENDATIONS

Starting your implementation for digital engagement requires careful planning, a lot of thought, dedication and, most of all, a significant investment of time. So it's important to understand the different strands you need to think about when you create your plan. There are several things that you need to consider when you build your community or ecosystem and make it self-sustaining and thriving. Imagine a citizenship project at your company. The project moves along defined tasks and timelines to a defined set of milestones. It is driven by one person, the project manager, who co-ordinates the rest of the team when required. But what if this project is driven by social networking? This project would engage volunteers for the project who felt that they had something to contribute. The volunteers would use their shared knowledge to come to a consensus about where the project was heading. Friends of the contributors, who also wanted to contribute, could also potentially work on the project, sharing their knowledge. The combined skills of the community of project workers would drive the outcome of the project.

Successful companies let customer feedback, based on experience and knowledge, drive their future direction.

> The three most important things that you need to make your project successful are community, content and connections.

You also need to listen to the community. Your customers are out there talking about you and your brand. It's very worthwhile listening to what they are saying. Listen to what they say about your brand, your products, and listen to their experience with you from a consumer point of view. Are they positive, neutral or negative towards you? Are they vocal in their praise about you? Are they detractors or, even worse, critics who influence others to become critics too? Without this level of market intelligence, you can run the risk of setting off in the wrong direction with your product and alienating your customers. Gaining product feedback from your customers in the form of online conversations is really important. You can elicit votes and comments on your website and you can ask questions.

> The answers that the community will give offer you a huge amount of information that rounds out your standard web metric results and will give you a different perspective for analysis and response.

Demonstrating to the customer that you are listening to them is important for your long term business goals and will allow you to create initiatives that will enable your business to grow and help to connect effectively with your customers.

Listen before you leap

This programme is a long term investment for your company and it will take some time before success and a positive ROI can be measured.

Starbucks listens to its customers and has produced some great results. Starbucks has a site called My Starbucks Idea (http://mystarbucksidea.com) where customers can suggest ideas to improve Starbucks. The site has polls where you can vote for your favourite kind of coffee or decide on a new initiative. Customers have persuaded Starbucks to sell Jamaican Blue Mountain coffee, sell decaffeinated iced coffee and bring back oatmeal and chocolate chip cookies. Since My Starbucks Idea launched in early 2008 Starbucks has had over 79,000 ideas submitted by the community, and the company has over 13 million friends on its Facebook page.

STARTING TO LISTEN

- Spending time collecting information about the audience before you embark on your customer engagement strategy is vital.

- The approach has to be communicated to your staff so that they can also become online advocates.

- Ultimately, your communications strategy will be embedded in your staff approach to customer engagement and it will become part of the values of your organisation.

Until that happens, the goals you set need to be realistic, flexible and focused on what your customers want. If the needs of the customer change, then the goals also need to change and it is important to bear this in mind when you create your plan.

Your trusted advisers

Referrals are really important when you are building your network of influencers and advocates. Just as a doctor may be asked whom he trusts when it comes to patient referrals, so **key people in your network will also be used by the community as super-referrers**. These super-referrers have a key set of good connections across several different networks, and information given to them has the potential to be spread broadly across a wide set of interconnected areas. These community members are very well connected, they are often first to try out a new product and they are considered to be influential amongst their groups. They are often not self-proclaimed experts, but they are genuine enthusiasts about their technology, and other members of the community go to them for thought leadership and trends. These leaders often have more reach and influence than traditional self-proclaimed experts. Experts already assume themselves to be thought leaders and often are not as interested in what others in the marketplace are actually doing. This makes them slower to adopt new practices, gadgets or technologies and slower to talk about them to others.

Beware the self-proclaimed experts.

You don't necessarily need to engage with the people who have the largest number of apparent connections. These people might not necessarily have the greatest number of strong relationships amongst their connections. Monitoring their blogs, status updates and forum entries will give you a good idea of how they interact within their social circle. Watching in this way will give you an indication of the strength of their networking ties and how many good strong and weak connections they have. These strong relationships will be more valuable to you as they indicate a trusted adviser status amongst their followers and friends.

Networks such as Twitter are useful for broadcasting ideas and discovering trends, but the word of mouth network is often hidden and poorly explored here.

Marketers have their work cut out to discover who maintains strong ties across their network and who propagates valuable and relevant information. Often marketing teams have relied purely on the number of connections that someone has and have not exploited the hidden links within a network. It's often the interaction between the 30 or so 'real' friends within a network that will bring the most value to the conversation.

You also need to consider the people who work inside your organisation.

Identify your existing evangelists, enthusiasts, pragmatists and any detractors you might have.

These are the people who might already be speaking publicly about your brand. Make sure you've prepared them to communicate externally with an effective, practical and workable social media policy. Give them training on the different types of tools that they will be using, remembering that tools that are in vogue today may be out of favour next year. Allow for change in your plans and make sure these are effectively communicated internally to the digital natives who will be contributors to your stream.

One of the most important benefits of effective engagement is the development of your 'voice'.

Whether this voice is the voice of yourself, the team, the organisation or the company, make sure that the voice is human. Leave the corporate style messaging to your PR team. The audience want to develop a relationship with you, your brand or your company in a way that isn't possible with structured PR messaging.

Try not to use any form of automated response. Just as auto-responders in email often irritate and turn customers away, so automated broadcasts will drive your followers away from your transmissions. To ensure that you create and maintain a strong relationship with your customers it is important to engage directly with your audience to give them that personal connection that they value. Investing in the personal touch will in time develop your relationship with them and will prove rewarding in diverse ways. Your connections will become your advocates, benefiting from being your first tier 1 influencers in your social graph, and having an indirect and positive influence on your sales.

If you want to improve your customer satisfaction ratings, reach out and engage with your customers. Regularly engaging with customers, quickly responding to their issues and engaging in open and honest dialogue will demonstrate a high level of customer care. This regular and personal interaction will start to alter customers' perceptions of you and your company.

CONSOLIDATING YOUR APPROACH

I was talking to a client about various different Web 2.0 options and I was going through various tools that she could use to complement her traditional marketing approach with an effective digital marketing strategy, and I was reviewing the different types of networks and tools that she could use to get started on her strategy. I mentioned Facebook and Twitter and ways to use each of these. 'Do I need to do both?' she asked. 'They seem very different.'

Facebook appeals to people looking to reconnect with old friends and keep up with the activities of family members or find new friends online. It also appeals to companies who wish to interact with their fans, offering them the chance to discover new products and services and engage in discussion with each other in a forum style environment. Twitter, on the other hand, encourages you to grab ideas in bite-size chunks and use your updates as pointers to other places on the web, or you can just let others know what you're up to at any given moment without any pointers or links. Dialogue is generally between the Twitter account holder and the person responding and there is less opportunity (and fewer characters) for a forum style discussion to take place.

On the surface, these seem to be completely different styles of applications. Facebook appears to nurture relationships and Twitter appears to broadcast news. But is this the case? Twitter certainly appeals to anyone who seeks the instant update or the news of the moment. Facebook, on the other hand, seems to group like-minded people together along common interests.

Twitter has the ability to move from simple real-time status updates broadcast to all, on to replies, retweets, direct (private) messages and finally on to face to face relationships. It's easy enough to initiate a conversation with people you follow on Twitter, who may then decide to follow you. This mutual following gives both of you the ability to send each other direct messages. Over time, as your relationship develops, your conversation can then progress to email,

Facebook, LinkedIn and ultimately face to face. The ability to add your Twitter feeds to Facebook means that you can connect different platforms together and streamline your updates.

Getting the cluster effect you need in your networks to grow your digital engagement efforts is fairly easy if all of your users have access to the same platform. Unfortunately the sheer variety of networking platforms can cause problems when trying to connect different networks together. Currently it doesn't matter which browser you happen to use on a day to day basis, you can still access your usual networking sites like Facebook, MySpace, LinkedIn and Twitter. This allows your network to grow and clusters of connections to be formed, regardless of operating system, regardless of browser. You need these clusters to grow your network and you need network effects for your news to spread effectively across these different types of networks.

Syndication
If you feel overwhelmed by the amount of potential updates that you have to do for each of the Web 2.0 sites that you contribute to, then there are syndication tools that can help you broadcast across several networking platforms at once:

SAVING TIME THROUGH SYNDICATING

- The Twitter Notifier is an add-on for Live Writer, an offline blog authoring tool. It can be configured to update Twitter every time you publish a blog post. It also provides a shortened URL so that Twitter followers can click the link to reach your blog.

- There is a Facebook application for Twitter which can update your Facebook status with each Twitter update you make. This can be found by searching Facebook for 'Twitter' and installing the application.

- You can update Twitter from Facebook. Search for 'Twitter updater' from within Facebook and install the Facebook application.

- LinkedIn has the ability to pull Twitter updates to display in your LinkedIn feed and can be configured from within the profiles setting area.

- http://ping.fm can update multiple networking sites at once from one status update. The application just needs to know the login credentials for each site you wish it to update.

Facebook Connect was introduced by the developers at Facebook and it pioneered the ability for website developers to access Facebook visitors' social graph information. Social graph information includes information about the users themselves, the users' friends, their status updates and other personal information stored on Facebook. This information is initially accessed by the application when the user explicitly authorises the application to use personal data.

> Applications can access all of your information to display actions and other details on the Facebook news feed.

For example, the Farmville application on Facebook publishes data about the farmer's progression through Farmville by publishing updates on the user's main status feed. Incentives, such as the offer of a free gift or bonus, can be used to entice friends of the farmer to also play Farmville. Incentives like this appearing on your profile page can encourage your friends to join in the game and lead to the acquisition of a greater number of players in the game for the application. Facebook Connect can be used in other ways too. Profile information, photos and other data such as birthday information can be used to deliver a more personalised experience to the user's status feed. Other applications can use the presence information provided by Facebook to take advantage of instant interaction and engagement between Facebook users.

Twitter has an authentication mechanism, Oauth, which allows single login across applications. You can create synergy with your updates across different types of applications and you can get interaction from people across networking platforms.

> Applications communicate with Twitter using a secure application channel to validate credentials.

Your login credentials are cached if you allow the application access so you don't need to maintain separate login details for both applications. This approach can be valuable to the community who can keep interacting with the tool of their choice whilst maintaining the connection across different applications.

YOUR EXISTING BRAND

It's fairly easy to find out what people are saying about you online. All you need to do is type your name into Google and have a look at the results. If you sign up for an alerts service like Google Alerts, Windows Live Alerts, Yahoo! Alerts or Bing News Alerts, you can get a daily digest about what is being said about you or your brand. If you have a blog there are search engines like Technorati or BlogPulse which specifically search through 200 million or so blogs and give you references to your name or other search terms that have been used on other blogs. Again, this is a useful way to find out who is talking about you – especially if there are no physical links or trackbacks to your blog from the originator's blog.

Most of the new interactive applications have search facilities for you to gauge the mood and sentiment of the social media landscape. Facebook, LinkedIn and Twitter all have search tools so you can find out what is being said about you or your brand. Twitter and most of the third party clients that connect to its application programming interface have search facilities. Twitter allows you to search for and retrieve a list of historical tweets for your hashtag, phrase or user name (Figure 8.1).

Figure 8.1 Twitter search

Searching for your brand in this way can give you an immediate sense about how your customers feel about you and lets you listen to their feedback, good or bad, about your company. It's a good idea to regularly search for your product name, brand or company so that you can see what people are saying about you, identify changes in almost real time and, more importantly, have the opportunity to change customer perceptions based on your early actions and response.

Preserving your online reputation

As you already have an online presence on the web, with an established personal or corporate brand you will already have some sort of online reputation. You may think that it's not relevant to you at all, but in the Web 2.0 world everyone has an online reputation, whether they realise it or not. Hopefully your online reputation is good at the very least. It would be nice to know if it's neutral, upsetting if you find that it's negative and absolutely devastating if it's vilified or targeted by cyber bullies. So it's important to consider how you can preserve your online reputation, especially as perception about you can change almost instantly.

The first thing that you could consider is to preserve your brand name. Take a popular enough name like that of my husband, Steve Brown. Typing his full name into the address bar returns a URL which redirects me to another site selling various things. Someone else has thought of registering his name like this before we have. They have registered the domain name http://SteveBrown.com and they are trying to make some revenue from someone who would like to purchase it – like him, or other Steve Browns across the world.

These names need to be registered on a long term basis with a domain hosting company. If you can manage to, try to purchase domain registrations for periods of longer than 2 years. After all, you're not intending to change your name (unless you're female and intending to change your maiden name when you marry). Securing your domain on a long term basis will ensure that no one else will be able to 'brand-jack' your domain name if you forget to update the registration. If you have several corporate products which have brand identities in their own right, then it's a good idea to register these too. There may also be trademarks which need to be considered in a corporate environment and registered with the appropriate trademark authority.

This all seems very innocuous so far, and only applies to someone who wants their own personally named domain. Imagine the problems that might arise if you were famous, in the media, or politics and someone was cyber squatting on your name. What if your name URL redirected to a very 'unsuitable' site, and even worse, the fake 'you' sites were turning up top of all of the search engines? What can you do to try and rectify things?

One of the best ways to be proactive about this is to buy all of the combinations of your name as domain names – including the unsavoury versions. So for our Steve Brown site example you could also buy:

> http://SteveBrown.net
>
> http://SteveBrown.org
>
> http://SteveBrown.co.xx

You could also consider purchasing other combinations of the name that you can think of – even the domains that are 'seedy', abusive, or unsavoury. So you might buy:

> http://SteveBrownS***s.com
>
> http://F***SteveBrown.com

and similar names.

Once you've secured the domain names use one of your registered names to start to build your positive online reputation. You could start to publish a blog on the domain. Wordpress and similar blogging platforms offer a simple way for you to redirect your own domain name to their website. If you want a website that is optimised for search engines (SEO) you need to make sure that you update the site often so that the web crawlers find fresh and updated content on a regular basis. Try to blog regularly in small manageable chunks so that the site is fresh and updated with frequent posts.

The search engine spiders will begin to crawl your website or blog, they will find updated content on it, and the spiders will start to visit it more regularly. Slowly, with diligence, your site domain name will rise up the page ranks and the site that you don't actually own will slowly move down onto the second page of search results where people hardly ever look.

> Pointers to your blog or website with fresh content will take precedence due to your regularly updated fresh content.

It will take some time to achieve this, but eventually you'll be able to recover your position in the search engine rankings with positive messages about your site which will improve perception about your reputation. Remember: prevention is always better, and cheaper, than cure.

Damaging your reputation

On Facebook, or MySpace, if you have created pages for your brand, you might want to consider the security settings on the application. You may not wish to have inappropriate content posted on the page of a friend of a friend and find that the content is linked to your page and tarnishing your reputation. It only takes a few moments for your reputation to change. Humorous behaviour can also do reputational harm. Early in 2010 the UK suffered from an extended and unprecedented fall of snow which paralysed the country for several days. Police officers in Oxfordshire,[44] wearing their high visibility jackets, were filmed using their riot shields to sledge down a snowy hill. It all seemed like fun, but these officers they were on duty. These videos were filmed using a mobile device which had the ability to immediately upload to YouTube. The viral nature of YouTube ensured the propagation of the links until it reached the eyes of the media, which took a dim view of their antics. Were their actions fun or irresponsible? Had the snow 'brought out the child' in them, or did the policemen overstep the mark? The decision is yours.

> The community decides and the power of the people has the ability to quickly change perception one way or the other.

When Steve Jobs was allegedly rushed into hospital with a heart attack, Apple's stock plummeted. In October 2008, bloggers reported that Steve 'claimed to be suffering from chest pains'. The story had started on a site which was linked to the CNN network. Apple PR categorically denied[45] the unfounded rumours. With citizen journalism, unsubstantiated rumours, **and no validation from the company itself**, there were a few upsets. Apple's stock took a tumble, CNN's credibility was in question in the media, and a Silicon Valley insider was heavily criticised for reporting on the story in the first place.

Sharing too much on Facebook

I've always smiled at the phrase 'What goes on tour, stays on tour', and I'm sure that lots of us could share some stories if that sentence had never been uttered. However, in this world of digital connections, mobile phones with cameras and immediacy, I think we need an updated version:

> What goes on tour stays on Facebook.

Facebook, with almost 600 million users, is growing at a fantastic rate. It took less than 9 months to add more than 100 million users to Facebook and there are over 1.5 million pieces of content shared daily. Some of this content isn't suitable for viewing outside your immediate network, but it all too often slips through.

> With Facebook's friendly interface and connections to your friends and family it is often easy to forget that it is a public website with extensions to your connections.

Unfortunately, Facebook can be much more public than you realise. Some Facebook users publish information that should often be kept private. Your own Facebook privacy settings may ensure that no one outside your immediate family can see your photos or your status updates, but there is nothing to stop any one of your friends taking a screenshot and broadcasting your message more broadly. There are hundreds of examples of foolish status comments that have been propagated by email, blogged about and propagated as a .jpg screen clipping throughout the web.

Sixteen-year-old Kimberley Swann, who worked at Ivell Marketing and Logistics at Clacton on Sea, Essex, posted comments on Facebook complaining about her job from the first day she started work.

> first day at work. omg (oh my God)!! So dull!!
>
> all i do is shred holepunch n scan paper!!! omg!
>
> 'im so totally bord!!!

Unfortunately her boss found her comments on Facebook, called her in to his office and terminated her employment. He said: 'Following your comments made on Facebook about your job and the company we feel it is better that, as you are not happy and do not enjoy your work, we end your employment with Ivell Marketing & Logistics with immediate effect.'

Crystal Bell was fired via Facebook, according to the *Kelowna Daily Courier*. She had been working for Faces Cosmetics & European Day Spa in Kelowna, she had missed a meeting on her day off and didn't call her boss to tell her.

> It's a good thing I checked my Facebook (site). I had one new message, so I went in and found that I had been fired by my boss.
>
> Her message to me said she found it very unprofessional that I didn't call and say I wouldn't be at the meeting, and that I should find another job.
>
> Firing someone on Facebook is not a professional way to do it.

Large companies also take a firm stand when finding out about indiscretions by their staff. Virgin Atlantic sacked 13 members of staff after they referred to their passengers as 'chavs', a term referring to their perceived social standing and intelligence.

> Following a thorough investigation, it was found that all 13 staff participated in a discussion on the networking site Facebook, which brought the company into disrepute and insulted some of our passengers. ... It is impossible for these cabin crew members to uphold the high standards of customer service that Virgin Atlantic is renowned for if they hold these views.

Direct complaints on Facebook aren't the only way to lose credibility. Status updates showing passive-aggressive behaviour can also be detrimental. Passive aggressive messages can include comments such as:

> I love it when the client cancels our meetings.
>
> It's fantastic when one of my customers think that they have exclusive rights on my time.
>
> Why can't the support team be more helpful?

If you have a public persona for your team or company, people will know if you're talking about them, even obliquely. They could imagine that you're talking about them and become concerned about your hidden meaning. Facebook status updates are not the best place to vent your frustration. Your reputation and credibility will suffer and you may turn clients away. Being negative online has far reaching effects and as your customer engagement goal is to try and grow your business, and improve perception, refraining from being rude or belligerent is a very good idea. It's easy to destroy your reputation with a few ill chosen words. It's also very difficult to discover the source of some reputation attacks as some choose to hide their true identities when launching an attack.

Cloning and faking your identity

Identity fraud is distressing enough for the individual, but what would you do if your brand was being cloned and used to execute business on your behalf? Your website could be copied and used for illegal purposes, or used as a phishing site specifically designed to extract confidential, personal or financial details from the unwary user. Banks often have to deal with these issues as copied sites are hard to distinguish from the genuine article and unwary users can be tricked into sharing personal details. You might have a significant customer satisfaction issue and poor perception about your brand or the security of the website through no fault of your own. People may also impersonate you when playing MMORPGs such as World of Warcraft, perhaps to gain status, award points or to damage your own standing in the game.

Designer labels have long been victims of piracy, with fake versions of designer items, usually produced in the Far East, appearing across Europe at cut down prices, but fake websites also abound to trick the unwary. Ugg boots are favoured by celebrities and mere mortals alike. They are sold in physical shops and also increasingly found online on websites and on eBay. Unfortunately there are also a lot of websites that offer fake Ugg boots. These are of inferior quality, and customers have complained about them. This poor quality fake merchandise has done damage to Ugg's reputation. Ugg has been proactive in stamping out fake websites that pretend to be genuine Ugg websites selling genuine boots. Ugg Australia has a page on its website advising what you can do in order to purchase genuine Ugg boots and works with customs agencies and Internet service providers to stamp out instances of fake shipments and cloned websites.

Corporations such as banks now have stringent processes in place to search out fake copies of their websites which are used to phish information about bank accounts for fraudulent use. Generally these fake websites appear as hyperlinks on a phishing email, which, when clicked, direct the unwary to a copy of the original banking website, ready to receive your data. Once a fraudulent site is uncovered, there are several procedures in place to remove the DNS record for the site so the DNS name no longer resolves to an IP address at the website. There is also a process for longer term disputes over websites names. The Uniform Domain-Name Dispute-Resolution Policy (UDRP) can resolve disputes over Internet domain name registration. The policy applies to .biz, .com, .info, .name, .net, and .org top-level domains. It can also include some country code top-level domains and the UDRP can be engaged to act on your behalf if the domain name in question is identical or similar enough to be confused with a trademark or service mark owned by another company and the registered domain name is being used it 'bad faith'.

Preventing online identity theft

There are some precautions you can take, however, to try to prevent identity theft. To completely avoid identity cloning on a personal level, you need to be extremely cautious when you are on the web. Make sure you remain aware of your transactions and activities, and you need to always protect your personal information. Here are a few ideas you could consider:

Use different passwords for each online site you use, and don't use sequential passwords to avoid phishing attempts on one site using the same or sequential logon details across other social networking sites that you use (LemonApple42, LemonApple43, LemonApple44 for example).

Use complex passwords with mixed case letters, numbers and a non-alphanumeric character. A good example is to use passwords that are not related or are not proper names. For example, you could use the first character of each word in a sentence to create your own acronym. Take the poem: 'Mary had a little lamb; its fleece was white as snow'. This would produce the following set of letters for your password:

Mhall,ifwwas

Use numbers to replace certain letters. You might use 1 instead of the letter l, 3 instead of E and 4 instead of H. Your original acronym becomes following complex password:

M4all,1fwwas

This makes your memorable sentence and the process to create your password process logical. It makes complex passwords easy to create and easy to change especially if you have a long piece of text to draw inspiration from. Adding non-alphanumeric characters like %, & * ! ; ^ makes the password even more difficult to guess.

You can change your birth date. When you register on a website consider adjusting your birth date so that it is one or two days different from your actual birthday. You could adjust the year of your birth by a year or so. If your actual birth date is needed, the website will probably have a mechanism where a manual check, performed by a human, will highlight the difference and contact you to confirm the real date. The only slight irritation of changing the date of your birthday may be that your friends will send you birthday wishes on a different day than your real birthday. This is a small price to pay for knowing that your true date of birth does not appear on any website and your real identity cannot be used for other purposes.

You can never be totally safe from identity theft or cloning, but if you put as many challenges as possible in the way, you can help to mitigate this risk.

Now we're online and active. We're going to find our audience and search for the job or that candidate that we really want to find. Let's now start to really publicise our online presence!

SUMMARY

- Discoverability is key to online success.
- Learn the behaviours that are important to user interaction and engagement.
- Listen to the community.
- Set goals based on what your customers want.
- Find your experts who have a true passion about what you do.
- Beware the self proclaimed experts.
- Use syndication to cross walled garden sites.
- Develop your voice.
- Use search facilities to check for information about your brand.
- Take steps to preserve your online reputation.
- Try to mitigate the risk of online identity theft.

9   DISCOVERY

'Create a community and it will come'. This is a great idea, and your community will come – however, they will only come if they know where they can find you. Your brand, both personal and corporate, needs to be discovered and needs to be advertised. In this chapter, we will look at ways to improve your search engine rankings through the intelligent use of social tools, and the need for you to keep active in online circles. We'll talk about how recruitment has been turned on its head, both from the ease of finding a role online, and the visibility that you have to potentially millions of recruiters. We'll find out how innovative use of social media has managed to put a whole musical orchestra together and we'll see how important the extended social network now is to recruiters and companies alike. We'll give some tips to think about if you're looking for a new role and want to try a different channel to publicise your skills, and we'll learn from recruiters and what they look for when they search for candidates.

We'll talk about how to grow your online audience and how you can find friends to connect with across different social networks. Finally, we'll look at how you can increase the number of connections you have and some techniques you could try for extra reach to your connections in your next digital marketing campaign.

CREATING AND PUBLICISING YOUR BRAND

What makes software popular? For many it's the feature set of the product. But now perceptions have changed, and this is entirely due to the new way we interact with each other online. Different types of websites attract different types of visitors. Features, interactive widgets and animations are designed to attract and entice. Early adopters, techies and enthusiasts will go to a site for different reasons than mainstream followers. One of the main reasons why you will visit social networking sites is that your friends, colleagues and people in your immediate network are engaging with their friends and interacting there.

> Having your contacts grouped together amplifies the network effect and significantly extends your potential reach.

The ability to connect outside your immediate network to include people further out in your social graph is important. These second degree connections can significantly add to the spread of networking and adoption of the site or application. You have your connections to your friends and you wish to extend your network outside your immediate circle of friends. You want to find those useful connections and work them into your network. LinkedIn, Facebook and Twitter all have search facilities where you can find others who are interested in the same things as you, whether in business, personal, political or scientific. You can connect directly or get connected through one of your first degree networks.

If you want to use the community approach to gather new connections, then you can use broadcasts to find your audience. Your audience are people who are interested in the same things as you are. If you blog, tweet, or update your networking sites regularly then others who are searching for similar topics will find your postings. With regular broadcasts and responses to your audience you will start to generate a relationship with your audience that will bring you more followers, extend your network and create potential new advocates for your brand.

As soon as you publish online, you'll get some kind of audience. But who are they? A lot of them are silent lurkers, they are visitors to your site who may have stumbled across your information accidentally and then move away. These visitors may be invisible to your eyes, they spend their time watching and waiting for you to connect with them. These lurkers are waiting for some information that resonates with them. It's hard to connect with these people if you don't know who or where they are.

You do know that these people are out there watching and listening, so there are things you can do.

> Consider adjusting your 'voice' to a different style to try to reach the people you don't currently know about.

If your style consists of opinions and commentary, you might want to try a different tone, such as information sharing, or questioning your readers. Your message has the potential to become diluted or taken out of context. It may be replicated elsewhere through different channels or it may not be replicated at all. There's always a chance that you won't connect with your original intended audience. Persistence always pays off, and it's worth bearing in mind that some people will never connect with you no matter how hard you try. Don't be disheartened. If you make sure that your site can be discovered easily by your audience, eventually the interaction will come.

Getting your website discovered requires some tweaking so that search engines like Google can find and index the site. Search engine optimisation, the art of improving the ranking of a website in search results, has been around for some time. Using keywords or meta-tags on your web pages can get your page higher up the search engine rankings, or get you some 'Google juice'. It's simple enough to use intelligent keywords, image keywords and keyword hotlinks on your web page. SEO specialists can register your site on search engines so that the spiders and search bots come to visit your page, but these are manual processes.

Fortunately, with the advent of status updates and online profiles, Web 2.0 techniques can improve your rankings with very little effort. User generated updates by their nature are dynamic, and having dynamic, frequently changing information on your site is a good thing. Dynamic updates ensure that web bots will visit your site more frequently and improve your rankings across the search engines. Google Bing and Yahoo! now index social media updates such as those from Friendfeed, Twitter and YouTube, so your recent communications on these sites can appear in the results fairly quickly. There are other considerations for SEO and practices you could put into place to publicise your brand or profile.

PUBLICISING YOUR BRAND

- Try to have a consistent naming strategy. If your company is called Best New Media Marketing Ltd, try to find a name that matches across all of your profiles. If you're going to use this name as your alias on Twitter, with its 140-character limit, you'll need to use short status messages as you won't have many characters left in the message.

- Try to reserve your brand identities by registering them. Use http://namechk.com to check whether the username you wish has already been registered on other networking sites.

- Think about your brand attributes. Are you reliable, efficient, dynamic, energetic, innovative, strategic, structured or creative? Make sure you include these attributes whenever you post online updates.

- Make sure your visual image portrays the brand you want, both in your corporate identity and your personal brand online. Consider whether using a headshot in your profile is the best for your brand, or whether your logo is the image you want your customers to see.

- Decide on your personal and professional brand limits. Decide where to draw the line. With suitable privacy settings, lock down any settings that you don't want broadcasted.

- Focus on quality and consistency in your message. Remember content is king and freshness is queen.

- Post information regularly. Find a schedule which works for you and stick to it. Whether you have the time to update once a day, or once a week, the key message is consistency. Avoid bursts of activity which will confuse the web crawl spiders and turn your readers away.

- Create channels for your brand. YouTube and Slideshare are just two examples of channels that you can customise with your logo and configure a background to the page in your company style. Facebook pages and LinkedIn groups, when well configured and maintained, promote your brand and encourage dialogue with your customers and partners.

- Cross-link. Refer to your Twitter feed, your Facebook page, your blog or your LinkedIn Profile on each of your sites so that each of them can be accessed from the other. If you want a single destination point, make sure that all of your profiles point to that site.

- Vary the content. Talking about the same thing using the same URL time after time will make your updates appear to be spam and your followers will go elsewhere.

- Keep the content on message. If your business is about ballet shoes, then make sure that the term 'ballet shoes' appears regularly in your blog posts, or on Twitter. You'll eventually turn up in search results for 'ballet shoes' if you regularly post ballet related updates on each of these sites.

- Comment on other blogs. Your comment profile will appear as a URL on the other blog site which links back to your site. Web crawl spiders will notice the links and give your site more relevance and ranking amongst other similar sites.

- Be generous with your links to other blogs which will draw traffic back to your site.

- Use several platforms and remember that you can link each of these. Content goes across most of these platforms.

The key thing is to make sure that the content is fresh and updated regularly. Appearing at the top of search engine results is not something that happens overnight. If you are diligent and organised about creating fresh content, then you'll be surprised at how quickly this can happen, and you can measure your success in weeks instead of months.

USING SOCIAL MEDIA FOR RECRUITMENT

Finding a job and recruiting for a role can be daunting and a huge time sink. You need a plan to market yourself and a plan for your approach.

Consider marketing yourself in the same way that you would market the feature set for a new product.

This approach can bring benefits. You can become innovative and creative in your search for a job. Adding digital media activities to your job finding pipeline can extend your reach and improve your chances. It certainly worked for one job hunter. Alec Brownstein is a copywriter who was looking for a new role with a creative agency. He went about it in an unusual way by purchasing Ad Words on Google for the creative directors' names he wished to target.[46] When they Googled their names, his ad appeared at the top of the list. He was offered two jobs.

Having an online presence which states your capabilities in a positive way can expose you to a potentially unlimited number of potential employers. Streamline your profile so it is seen by your target audience, and focus their attention on your key skills.

Social networking sites allow you to segment your interests. You can join specialised groups focusing on your specific interest, skills and aspirations. These specialised groups are followed by your intended audience and thus anyone searching for skills in a particular area is more likely to find you there. LinkedIn is an excellent example of this, with almost half a million groups to choose from on politics, technology, recruitment, networks – anything, really, as you can easily create your own group which is searchable from within the groups directory. You can easily find specialised groups on Facebook too, and YouTube categorises its videos for easier searching.

A new way to find a job

YouTube has been used to successfully recruit a specialist band of people. In February 2009 musicians from around the world were invited to audition exclusively using YouTube as the medium.[47] They were asked to upload a video of themselves playing a segment from a piece of music. These videos were voted on by YouTube viewers around the world. The winners were selected to play at Carnegie Hall in New York in April 2009 under the direction of Michael Tilson Thomas. A mashup video was created of the event which is also on YouTube. Jim Moffat, who played French horn in New York, said about his experience:[48]

And so to my own romantic foolishness, an attempt, courtesy of the YouTube Symphony Orchestra virtual auditions, to create a decent rendition of one movement of Mozart's earliest horn concerto – commonly known as the second. It was maddening. I discovered how to create semi-watchable video and passable audio, in my dining room. And how to concentrate for five minutes, never an easy task. There I stand, naked but for my underwear. You may see with your eyes a man relaxing in a comfy cricket jumper, but hear with your ears a man starkers.

Finding a job using social tools is not as easy as joining a new networking site and announcing 'Give me work'. You need to build up your reputation and your online profile so that your connections can get to know and trust you. Your profile needs to be comprehensive, clear and concise. Start connecting, link to others who have the same interests as you. Respond to queries, make recommendations to people you've connected with, make new connections and keep existing connections alive with communication and interaction.

Once you've created your profile, you need to keep it fresh so that your changes continue to appear on the pages of your connections. You might like to change something on your profile every few days to alert your followers to new content. If you're using a tool like LinkedIn to manage your profile and connections, every modification you make to your profile shows up in others' timelines and draws their attention towards you if you have allowed this on your privacy settings. Update your status regularly so that recruitment agents know that you're looking for new opportunities.

Your second level connections are also important to you. These are the people who have a greater social distance from you. Your immediate network may not be able to help you but **their** networks might have the answer you need.

The 'friend of a friend' network can prove to be an extremely powerful asset to you.

The connectors and key networkers in your immediate networking circle may be very useful to you in recommending you to one of the connections in their network. If you start to build up your own valuable connections and develop a good relationship with them, you'll find that your extended network grows significantly and can have great potential.

Searching for jobs
If you're searching for a new job, you need to have a good online presence and brand. Your online brand is the first thing that recruiters will search for when they want to check out your credentials. Publicising your profile online is a great and free way to advertise your ability and build your brand. You can use some of the techniques I've mentioned to find your perfect role. Now that you know that recruiters are looking out for you, it's really important to tidy up all of your online profiles to make sure you give the right impression to your potential new employer.

FINDING A JOB

- Most recruiters turn to LinkedIn first to check out details of your CV, so make sure that your LinkedIn details match the CV that you submitted to the agency.

- Ensure your LinkedIn profile is 100% completed. If your LinkedIn profile is sitting at 75% and you're sure that you have completed all of the fields, you need to get recommendations about your recent work from your connections. Recruiters want recent testimonials about your work, so make sure these referrals are up to date.

- Make your LinkedIn public profile name easy to remember. For example, http://LinkedIn.com/in/eileenbrown is much easier to remember than http://uk.linkedin.com/pub/eileen-brown/2/5b7/978. It's easy to change the URL in your profile settings.

- Link your online accounts to each other and link them to LinkedIn. If you link your Facebook account to LinkedIn, make sure that you have your appropriate privacy settings in place to avoid any personal data migrating onto your professional page. If you use Facebook for entirely personal reasons, then protect your Facebook profile and don't link it to LinkedIn.

- Search for job-specific keywords on Twitter, Google and Facebook. Recruiters may be advertising for roles on these sites using the same phrases. Use the RSS feed functionality of Twitter to save any tweets that appear to your RSS reader for action at a later stage. Set up Google Alerts for job-specific words.

- Post your CV online if you're openly looking for a role. You could create a link to your curriculum vitae on your blog or you could create a visual CV on Slideshare if your speciality is in design. Syndicate it across your other network sites so that everyone is aware of it.

- Search for your target keywords on LinkedIn. Someone may be advertising your dream role.

Be active, consistent and current in these areas. You and your online profile will bubble up to the top of the search results and your second degree network might turn up the role designed specifically with you in mind.

Recruiting from social networking sites

As a recruiter, if you don't use sites with a high degree of audience engagement and conversation to find candidates you may be missing out on some top notch candidates who do use these types of sites to find their next role. Advertising on job boards gives you access to half of your potential candidates, telling your story on as many sites as possible, and actively searching out candidates will significantly broaden your horizons.

> The purpose of social networking in a business context is to engage with others. If you are not using social media, you will never know who else is out there.

Regularly advertising your presence on Twitter using keywords can bring benefits, and if requests are phrased appropriately, you can avoid the flood of inappropriate CVs. Anyone doing keyword searching will find you and your job. Many human resources professionals who aim to recruit use sites like LinkedIn and Facebook, not only to check out your employment history but also to look for your recommendations from your previous employers. According to a survey of human resources professionals, over 48% spend more than 3–5 hours per week searching for suitable candidates whom they otherwise wouldn't know or couldn't contact.

Cisco uses this form of communication very effectively as a recruitment tool and to communicate with and engage Generation Y. Cisco EMEA (Europe, Middle East and Africa) conducts graduate recruitment through Facebook groups and has a very successful master page with over 4,000 fans. There are three pages pertaining to EMEA: a high level graduate recruitment page, 'Cisco Graduate Recruitment', with other groups such as 'Emerging Markets East' – Middle East region, and the CIS region. Cisco provides information on upcoming campus events, and offers programmes and opportunities for graduates across various disciplines. The team respond to questions related to the overall graduate recruitment process and discuss graduate roles on the pages. Fresh content and activity on the page keep the page activity growing. One of the benefits of having a Facebook page with so many fans is that Cisco then has the opportunity to check out potential candidates if it chooses to.

Executive search agencies and consultants use tools like LinkedIn to trawl through profiles, searching on phrases like 'looking for new opportunities'. You won't be able to guarantee a good hire, but if you're smart about your use of searches, and make good use of the resources out there, then you'll get a very good idea of the available talent. A key benefit of using sites such as LinkedIn is that you can ask those in your LinkedIn network if they know of anyone in **their** network who might fit your criteria. This allows you to take advantage of your extended network, the second degree connection. The candidate may not be suitable for a role offered by your colleague, but they may dovetail perfectly into the role you're trying to fill. Take advantage of your second degree network, it could bring you unexpected benefits.

It's a good idea also to check whether anyone already on your shortlist has a presence on sites that you may not be aware of. Technorati will find blog entries, Google or Bing will find tweets, email addresses and entries posted on other social networking sites that you may not be aware of. You may find evidence of skills that didn't make it onto the candidate's CV. This may be due to space constraints on the original document, but it can give you a different insight into the candidate. Perhaps your candidate does charity or pro bono work, perhaps he leads communities or interacts with a wide circle of influencers, and perhaps he has published papers online.

When you are considering a candidate you can check sites for the candidate's writing style, patterns of behaviour, grammar, spelling and general attitude. You also have the opportunity to see what other people are saying about your candidate online, and have a look at their interaction on Twitter. Lots of the under 30 age group tend to favour Facebook over LinkedIn, using Facebook for their social and business interaction, so be sure to look there. If you happen to find an unsuitable photo of your candidate, don't necessarily rule her out completely. Her transgression may have been simply a one-off which her other entries on different sites show to be out of character. You can, however, get a feel for her other activities from online profiles that may not be obvious at first look. There may be drug and alcohol use or abuse, a poor attitude to work in general, negative feelings about a former employer or humorous stories about missing work. These clues can add to the general impression, good or bad, of a candidate and help you effectively refine your choice.

Social networking sites will never replace the recruitment screening process entirely, but they will help you to reduce some of the legwork required, circumvent some of the questions, and gain a great understanding about your potential new hire.

DISCOVERING THE INFLUENCERS IN YOUR AUDIENCE

If you're intending to market your product or services using conversational media, then you need to identify the correct part of your audience, and find who your influencers are. Depending on the type of business you're in, your audience and potential customers are active in their own specific spheres. They may be decision makers inside the firewall, they may not hold budget themselves, but they may have significant influence over the decision makers at your customer. Your influencers may be key technologists in the community, considered trusted advisers in their field. They might be geeks who are visionaries in your industry, they may be early adopters or trend setters. These people will help you advance your business, they will help in achieving a measurable ROI, and you would benefit from making them your friends.

Seeding these influential members of the audience with information is your challenge.

How can you ensure that these people are the hubs in their network and will extend your buzz across their own networks?

Traditionally marketers have looked for influencers who are active in a structured network, but research has shown that networks are often split into zones or smaller hubs within the network. The key to finding your influencer is not to search for the hub of the whole network.

> It's about finding the right individual who will spread the message across all of the different subgroups within a network.

These individuals, with their links to many subgroups, are known as **superconnectors**. These subgroups may be classified by technology, geography, interests or social activity, but careful examination will find those users who transcend these networks and, more importantly, link different networks together. To effectively market to these people, take a closer look at who these super-connectors are and who they communicate with regularly. Then you can start the discussion with the right connector.

Online 'friends' are very important. They will help you to expand your network beyond the initial circle of networking contacts you have. Like the six degrees of separation experiment where each person is one step away from each of their direct contacts and two steps away from their contacts' contacts, everyone on earth is theoretically connected by at most six steps.

> The important thing to remember is that these steps are not equal in strength. Some of your close friends are bound by extremely strong ties, and other casual acquaintances are connected to you by much weaker ties.

Social structures are modelled using both weak and strong ties, and it is often the case that weaker ties become stronger for a time, in order to perform some transient social function. This function might be something as simple as connecting you to one of their strong ties to form a bond. This system of social hubs and routing hubs, strong ties and weak ties, forms the basis of all connections. It is dynamic and fluid, and it changes all the time.

Finding your audience and friends

Hubs, people who have a collection of friends who feed them information, routers who pass information onto other hubs, and endpoints who receive output from hubs and routers are very useful in your network. However, you may want to discover easy ways to increase your audience. For example, you may be launching a new campaign and one of your metrics is to get 'net new' visitors to your site and increase your audience by driving page views to your target campaign site.

There are hundreds of social networks, some are specialised and designed for specific interests, and perhaps hobbyist or music sites, and some are more generic.

You may know and use LinkedIn for your business contacts and Plaxo to connect your email contact list to others. You might use Last.fm, MySpace, Pandora and Spotify for music, and Facebook, Hi5, Orkut and Twitter for your social connections.

> These websites are 'sticky', they are simple and popular, they encourage connections and they drive huge amounts of user engagement.

Users tend to spend a lot of time on their sites, they store a lot of their data on them, and there are tools such as Facebook that allow friends using different social networks to connect with each other. This amount of engagement means that there's a great opportunity here for advertisers to take advantage of these websites and connections. A simple example would be the opportunity for job search and recruitment companies to have a tight tie-in with LinkedIn. LinkedIn could display job advertisements targeted according to the user's online profile. There is also an opportunity for consumer brands to advertise across Facebook and YouTube, and opportunities to drive traffic to the website using Twitter updates – providing, of course that they have compelling and eye catching status messages.

There are many ways to automatically find new people to follow on Twitter via an array of tools which offer free and paid-for services.

> These services offer automated ways to gather new followers and ways to follow those who tweet about keywords you choose.

Several Twitter clients – including Tweetdeck, Seesmic and TweetGrid – allow search strings to be placed into a separate feed column to discover who is talking about your product, service or brand. Whilst this is a great opportunity to gather feedback, it still requires manual intervention to follow these people if you so choose.

Searching for the right information is easy. There are tools to help connect you to anything you want on the web, whether it's stored in a web page, a YouTube video or a blog. Tools like Technorati and IceRocket search blogs, while Yahoo! Search, Google and Bing search content on web pages and across social networking sites. MetaTube and Redlasso search for videos, and CrowdEye is used for social searches. Most of these tools offer targeted online advertisements, so there's a potential business opportunity to increase revenue on these sites.

> If you have a presence across several networks and you have fresh and interesting content, you'll be seen by your target audience. Some of your followers will link to you and their friends will notice this presence and amplify your message on your behalf.

Increasing your following

If part of your customer engagement strategy is to increase the number of your followers then you need to think ways to engage your new audience. The mechanisms for increasing followers are pretty much the same whatever tool you use, and whether you want to spread your message across the Twitterverse or score large numbers of hits for your YouTube video.

> Your strategy needs to consider the fact that once you've identified your audience, you need to get them to follow you or subscribe to you, so the most important thing here is to provide interesting content.

Your broadcasts need to have useful, relevant and informative information to capture their attention and keep them engaged. This information could be in the form of news about an upcoming event, a product or beta launch or a new piece of business news. It could be a simple 'how-to' article. I love the 'how to fold a t-shirt' videos on YouTube. These 'how-to' articles appear at the top of the search engines. Try it!

Whatever your information is, it needs to be useful enough for people to recommend it to their connections, who recommend it to their connections and amplify the message.

STARTING YOUR SOCIAL MEDIA PLAN

Unfortunately there are lots of poor quality campaigns and things can go wrong. Some marketers continually spam their followers with the same message over and over again. Adverts like 'Don't pay for tooth whitening. This Mom discovered the secret to white teeth for under $5' repeated across each of your sites will not give you the profile you desire. If the tooth whitening solution is one of the few products that you market, then you need to be creative about the different ways you can broadcast your message.

BROADCASTING YOUR MESSAGE

- Find the active conversationalists, influencers and leaders in your industry and follow them. Subscribe to their blogs, follow them on Twitter, and connect with the people they connect with. You'll then get great insights into the way they use online marketing to get their message across effectively.

- Search for the types of people you want to notice you and follow them. Use keywords to narrow your search to the target market. Comment on their blogs, photos and video uploads, link to them and follow them on Twitter. This will increase their reputation in the community and bring you to their attention.

If you follow people in your industry and post interesting things, it's likely that they will follow you back.

- Decide on a sensible name for your channels. People are much more likely to follow realistic companies like 'WhiteTeeth' than they are to follow channels such as 'Awesome Tooth Whitening Products'.

- Make sure your channels are populated. People won't subscribe to a blog that isn't updated regularly, nor will they follow a blank Twitter feed or an uninteresting YouTube channel.

- Try to broadcast realistically. If you insist on talking about your amazing tooth whitening products all the time, you will appear to be spamming your audience. Try instead to ask poll questions like 'Which tooth whitening product is your favourite?' or 'Which tooth whitening product would you try?' Your consumers are intelligent and will move away in droves from a poorly executed strategy.

- If your social media strategy centres around Twitter, make sure that you don't follow everyone. You will be overwhelmed with information and will miss out useful snippets in the fire hose of communication. Make sure that if you choose to follow lots of people on Twitter, then your Twitter client software allows you to create groups of key influencers, friends, and business associates, so you can filter out the noise.

- Post interesting news and information about your product, and advertise your message regularly. Also make sure that you also talk about other products to give yourself credibility across the market. Highlight news across your industry sector to show balance. If others post relevant and interesting news on Twitter, use the retweet function to broadcast this to your own followers. Re-share Facebook pages with your friends with interesting links and broadcast interesting video uploads. Use trackbacks to link to blogs with relevant content.

- Use URL shorteners so that your links can be forwarded easily. You might want to publicise a link on your blog, or on Facebook. Use one of the many URL shorteners to create a smaller link that people can easily share within Twitter's 140-character limit. If you use a shortener with metrics tracking facilities, then you can track the click-through numbers from the link.

- Search for your brand name on blogs, videos, and Twitter. Respond to any comments or questions. If there are any issues, then make sure that you try to get a solution for the customer. The customer will know you are listening, and their perception of your brand will improve.

Once you have been discovered, then you need to take advantage of your network of friends and your friends' friends. If you have a small team, or are attempting this yourself, then your next challenge is to think about scaling your network activities and working the crowd.

SUMMARY

- Group your contacts together to amplify the network effect.
- Have a consistent identity and broadcast pattern.
- Use LinkedIn for recruitment and to find a new job.
- Provide interesting and fresh content for your followers to find you.
- Plan the way you broadcast your message.

10 SCALING NETWORKS

Taking advantage of the opportunity to join in the great conversation isn't without its problems. If there are restrictions on your budget, headcount and time then it may be difficult for you to find the relevant people to help you extend your network. In this chapter we'll talk about engaging the right types of people to help you propagate your message, the sorts of rewards that motivate these people and how you can get them to become your advocates. We'll have a look at the different behaviours of different age groups on social networking sites and how they engage with their peers. We'll see how different ways of sharing data have evolved and the potential for community and enterprise mashups to be put to good use for both community and businesses. We'll also have a look at the differences of behaviour inside the firewalls.

> Inside companies, reticence in adopting the new way of communicating has resulted in huge amounts of data storage and ineffective collaboration, information islands and siloed data repositories.

We'll also look at opportunities to change this approach from the ground up and we will look at ways to change the way of working from the traditional 'top down' hierarchical approach. Finally, we'll look at how these tools have encouraged companies to use social media as a customer connections tool to gather market intelligence about their products. We'll explore how they can quickly respond to customers with problems and build effective relationships that validate the investment in their digital engagement activities. These activities will enable them to scale to a much greater level than their traditional customer service approaches currently do.

SCALING NETWORKS

It's all very well having a social media strategy, a plan to reach millions of potential new customers that will charm your army of advocates into buying your products, but there may be something niggling at the back of your mind. Scale. How on earth will you single-handedly reach such a large number of people? With IT departments stretched to breaking point with no staff to spare, this is going to be a challenge. You have limited budget, minimal time to invest in your carefully crafted 'execution policy' and no other resources at your disposal. You probably feel that this new edict from above is impossible to achieve. You can't implement your digital marketing strategy alone. Of course, if you consider yourself to be a sole trader or you are running a small business and have no other resources at your disposal then you might think that you have no other option.

However, there are potentially millions of helpers at your disposal. You could use this super-connected network of extended friends to build up a set of connections for you.

> These connections are not just a band of happy followers who love your product and buy every new version or revision that they can get their hands on.

These are your loyal football fans. They have the season ticket, they attend every match that they can – even the away games – and they buy all of your merchandise whenever a new club design comes out. But most of these 'football fans' stay silent – apart from when they're actually at a game of course. These followers do not actually help you get your word out to your new potential customers. They are the silent majority. These types of people will always buy the same brand of baked beans, toothpaste or tampons. They have done so for years and they don't intend to change on a whim.

> The problem with the silent majority is that they won't evangelise your product for you. For this you need to reach out and find your 'noisy few'.

The noisy few exist in your immediate network, your tier 1 network, and they are vocal. They may be positive, they may be negative, but they are communicating with you. They **want** to talk to you. All you need to do is connect with them and start a conversation. The noisy few will relish the opportunity to communicate with you. They will form a relationship and engage in regular discussions with you about your brand, product or feature set.

> Over time these noisy few will become your advocates, and your friends. Your noisy few will tell your story on your behalf.

OUR BEHAVIOUR IS INFLUENCED BY OUR AGE

The way that grownups have approached social media is totally different from the way their children use the tools. Adults don't tend to have free flow conversations with each other on your Facebook wall and they don't tend to send many virtual hugs. They don't tend to use quizzes to the same extent as the younger generation, nor do they join hundreds of groups and subgroups. They do tend to contact their friends with birthday wishes, they will comment on their friends' status messages, and they will click on the 'like' tag on Facebook. They will even 'favourite' a particular tweet on Twitter when something captures their interest. Their behaviours tend to be very different from their teenage children, and this behaviour even filters through to the way they use their profile information on their network.

Adult behaviour

Adults tend to complete their initial profile when they set up an account on a site. They use their profile primarily to promote their business; they add links to their website or blog. As far as the social aspect is concerned, they will display their hobbies and interests and they will complete most of the personal sections of their profile. Adults only tend to complete their profiles to a minimum level, presenting a minimal framework of their activities which becomes a permanent record of their account.

This is totally different from the way that young people treat their profiles. Teenagers' and young adults' online profiles are a living, breathing, organic record of their personality, mood and situation at that moment in time. Their status updates and their moods are frequently changed, often several times a day. They join numerous groups and interact and modify their home pages on the site.

Adults' use of social networking sites reflects exactly what these sites were originally intended for, which is primarily to connect and communicate with their friends from now, and from their past. The networking site, Friends Reunited, is a prime example of this online 'school reunion' where everyone can find out what happened to their classmates and work colleagues. They can communicate with old friends, comment on old enemies and rejoin the dots of their history.

Teenagers and social networking

For young people in the US, online services have become the place to go to socialise.

It's a little like the online version of the youth club, it is the place for people to congregate, gossip, agonise over teenage relationships, socialise and exchange information. The term networking, which tends to be used by adults in business environments, is not an alien term to young people.

They congregate in groups of friends they know and they tend not to reach out to new groups. However, they don't really need to socialise outside their immediate school or social group. If they use sites like Friendster, MySpace, Bebo and Facebook, they can exchange information, chat with their online friends, enhance their profile and customise their page to suit their personality. They can advertise the things they like, the books they read, and films they watch, and create lists of their favourite foods. They can take quizzes, adopt virtual names and personalities which they change on a regular basis and they can express themselves to the world. This social behaviour seems to help them prepare for the transition into adulthood; it's a type of social grooming amongst their peers that helps them to operate in the adult world whilst in the safety of their own social circle, with their own language, habits and social rules.

Teenagers use sites that allow them to interact within their social circle. They can update their status, they can join groups, and they can change their mood or their relationship status to alert their friends to what is going on right here, right now. They use emoticons to share the mood of the moment with their friends, not their parents. They are horrified that their parents are also on Facebook, though they might also connect with them or follow them on Twitter. This group of teenagers wants to hide certain things from their parents, whilst still telling all to their immediate social circle. They need to have a balance in information that is propagated.

I've seen blog posts that speculate that there aren't too many teenagers who use Twitter. Perhaps this could be due to the very public nature of Twitter, where your every status message can be seen, unless your profile is locked. The nature of Twitter encourages sharing information in a wide public forum. Perhaps teenagers prefer to grade their broadcasts to different groups, and the only way to hide your updates in Twitter is to secure the stream. This doesn't seem to be of benefit to the broadcaster who secures their status updates. Twitter is all about the broader conversation, and perhaps it appeals to an older age group. A Twitter update can potentially become a news item – as celebrities and politicians are increasingly finding out.

OTHER WAYS OF BROADCASTING YOUR MESSAGE

Video sharing

There are many ways to extend your brand using mechanisms other than the written word. YouTube, the second largest search engine after Google in terms of items searched, has over 100 million videos that you can search. Videos are created by corporate teams, film and video companies, end users, and now it is really simple to quickly upload a video captured on a mobile device. And there are many other video hosting and sharing sites too – Viddler, Vimeo, Hulu, Brightcove, MetaCafe, to name just a few. You can broadcast your video stream in real time too. Services like Ustream, BlogTalk radio and Justin.tv use livecasting, streamed video and tools for broadcasting in real time to your audience.

There are services that enable you to add telephone dial-in facilities to host a multi-party video conference. You can save the audio files or the video stream so that users can download the session as a compressed MP3 file at a later stage – ideal for any users that didn't get to hear the original broadcast. You also have the opportunity to upload documents to accompany the session. There are options in some of these tools for a Twitter stream to be embedded alongside the broadcast so that questions can be tweeted in for the presenters to answer. This instant delivery allows a host of opportunities for companies who can use video for educational services, training, product launches and PR campaigns. You can secure the channel to host your own private business meetings if you don't have a comparable conferencing solution in house.

Asics, the shoe company, created a video for YouTube about the origin of the company – all done using origami. The video quickly went viral with comments about the beauty of the video and the story of how the company was created. This viral video had a secondary effect. Within a few days of the video being posted, the company saw a huge upturn in traffic on the main Asics site and a much greater awareness of the brand.

Audio broadcasting

Podcasting (personal on demand broadcasting) has been around for a few years now and is very popular. It is really easy to download audio files from the web to listen to selected snippets of a radio show at your convenience. You can also create podcasts for use in learning and training, for capturing vox pops at events, and to record facts and narratives. These audio files are a good way for technical people to showcase their expertise in a specific area. This might be a series of podcasts documenting the Second World War in manageable session 'chunks' or it might be advice for people who need personal coaching to appear more confident. There seems to be podcasts for every conceivable subject. Podcasts can be placed on the web for anyone to download to their PCs or devices, or delivered via a specific service like podcast.com to specific users.

Currently one of the most popular mechanisms for listening to podcasts is Apple's iTunes, but there are other services such as Podbean and Rhapsody that you can use. One of the key advantages of podcasts is that they can be any length you want. This means that you can deliver short targeted broadcasts of a few minutes, with snippets of useful information, or record a series of lectures of an hour or more.

Let the community categorise the content

With the move away from structured taxonomies on the web and the wide adoption of folksonomies, much richer data can be tagged and found on the web. You can tag photos that you upload to photo sharing sites, in addition to naming them. This extra information gives applications a wealth of resources to take advantage of. Imagine a mashup, with a mapping service like Google Maps or Bing Maps. Users can visit a location and see photos of the area that have been taken by the community and uploaded to a photo sharing site like Flickr or Yfrog. Now imagine a 360-degree panorama of the area consisting of photographs that have been taken by different people and merged using photo stitching software. This technology already exists and has been demonstrated to great acclaim at the TED conference.[49] Imagine user-created videos attached to the location map so that upon looking at your destination you can take a virtual tour of the location and see it from the community point of view. It's a really powerful concept that brings social photo sharing into enterprise applications – and provides a great opportunity for website owners and advertisers to take advantage of.

The Landmark Trust, which lets out unusual buildings for people to stay in, doesn't have many pictures of its fascinating-looking properties. There are castles, lighthouses, gatehouses, forts and towers. However, visitors to the Landmark Trust have taken photographs of these amazing places and uploaded them to Flickr where they are tagged with the name of the property and also the tag 'Landmark Trust'. This is a great example of the community getting together, following no hard and fast rules for categorising these photographs, but using their own way of tagging to provide order and structure for the greater good.

INSIDE THE FIREWALL

Businesses may not yet be using social media in a structured way, but with the groundswell of adoption, especially amongst the Generation Y and Z crowd, the use of social tools in a business setting will become more and more widespread.

HOW GENERATION Y WORK

Generation Y are your future managers, executives and engineers, and their adoption of social networking methods for communication and collaboration will shape the next generation of communications platforms products and services. These people are 'prosumers'; they use social media, networks and any tool at their disposal to effectively and efficiently do their job.

This has a huge and far reaching impact on business. Industries that embrace this new world of work are enjoying success – look at how Dell have benefited by being agile in this area. Ultimately, for your business success, you need to be there too. There are huge opportunities created by word of mouth networks, and smart businesses see the need to collaborate in these areas where there are opportunities for marketing your products and brands. Collaboration inside the firewall is just one part of social networking.

Collaboration enables companies to exchange intellectual capital with colleagues inside of their company.

Corporations invest huge amounts of money in storage systems to store corporate data – but as soon as a file is stored on the corporate network, the data effectively dies. With poor enterprise search tools, this dead data is no longer a corporate asset; users spend more and more time trying to find the documents they need amongst the ever growing mass of data.

If you implement a system that enables effective and contextual search to discover the data, use meta-information to tag the content appropriately and add multi-user editing and version control, things change. This data becomes discoverable, updatable and, more importantly, alive. And it's the living data that becomes a strategic asset to a company and enables corporate agility.

Having live up-to-date documents instead of terabytes of archives can reduce the need for storing duplicate data. Your new, modified versions of the original documents are used from the document store, and document versioning keep the original version intact.

The term 'social media' conjures up images of tools like Twitter and Facebook and brings to mind their use and misuse on the Internet. Often companies are wary of opening ports to allow the use of social software inside the firewall because of the potential risks that it may bring. Companies either ban sites through use of firewall block lists, or they monitor usage through audit trails and policies. Restricting your staff from using these sites will drive them to communicate with their friends from their mobile devices, or use other WiFi networks to access the sites in their lunch breaks. But social networking applications can also be used to enhance efficiency and productivity inside companies. In this context it tends to be known by a different name: social computing.

Social computing: the new productivity
With the growing use of social computing within companies, users are starting to reap the benefits of enhanced productivity. If a company has implemented a productivity suite with a unified mechanism for collaboration then it can start to communicate in real time. If it has installed an application that can display a list of colleagues and show whether they are online, away from their desk or on the phone, then this information can also be embedded into other applications to provide dynamic information around the company. Staff can easily communicate with their colleagues using instant messaging without the need for email and the associated disk space. If they use and manage dynamic websites instead of static pages, they can take advantage of the knowledge capital that the business already has and keep their data alive. Collaboration offers significant value to companies, but without the dynamism offered by socially connecting, exchanging information and chatting with your friends, collaboration can only give value in one aspect of business life.

Social computing doesn't necessarily mean embracing Facebook, Twitter and MySpace inside the firewall. It's about using the collaboration tools you have in a new way. Using wikis for group work, or changing your intranet pages to wikis instead of static web pages, means that as data changes at the company, updating the system involves only a small amount of work. Adding document versioning and meta-information to your documents means that information can be discovered in a new way. Instead of searching for 'consultancy proposal for NHS', for example, you can search for 'NHS Surrey project management 2010' or 'server refresh Surrey hospitals'. This richer meta-information allows for more targeted searches and more relevant results which ultimately improve productivity.

Searching for information
The average user in a large company can spend up to 10% of their time searching for documents on the intranet, so implementing social computing can soon improve productivity. Adding presence information to the document repository and landing pages means that document authors can be contacted immediately to clarify any queries. Status updates and out of office messages can bring richness to intranet sites and encourage greater interaction.

In the short term, this new way of working does require a shift in behaviour. Think about how your team interacts at the moment. You might email documents around for review by the team, which can often cause bandwidth and mailbox issues if you send large files. You might call your team on the phone, leaving voice-mails, and then email them to follow up on your voicemail. You might have a set of file shares on the server where all of your project documentation is stored. Think about how much more productive you could be if you could only change the way the team works.

This shift in behaviour could lead to everyone in the team storing their documents in a dynamic way on the document management system. You could use instant messaging with presence information to see whether the person you want to talk to is at their desk. You could then start a conversation by instant message, switching to voice and adding video. You could work on the same document and save a copy of the amended document. You could collaborate with wikis and you could have information updated quickly by members of the team. In the long term, this behaviour will reap benefits to both the information workers and the company through increased productivity and efficiency. Businesses sometimes flinch when they contemplate allowing the use of these tools behind the corporate firewall, but a quick analysis of access logs shows that over 80% of web visits are to social sites such as LinkedIn, Facebook and Twitter.

Collaborating with your colleagues

The desire to communicate with colleagues and friends both inside and outside the firewall will set the direction for the organisation's social strategy. Tools can be incorporated as part of a bottom-up approach to implementing new working practices instead of the current top-down approach to information dissemination. You might consider having an email group that is used for social activities. These social activities could be notices about items to sell, company events, 'how do I?' type emails, and the group could soon grow to become a central repository of information. Microsoft in the UK has an email group for its campus staff. Over half the staff in the UK subscribe to the mailing list, it is policed by its members and it covers topics as diverse as warning drivers about traffic hold-ups on the M4, and advice to people not to go too close to the pond as the resident geese have hatched their new brood of chicks. It also acts as the pulse of the company staff to gauge mood and sentiment about any new initiative or idea that is introduced onto campus.

Companies that decentralise the passing of information like this become a community of individuals sharing and contributing to corporate knowledge. This leads to an enhancement of corporate intellectual property and an increase in connectedness of the silos of information stored across the company. Companies that adopt this approach are inherently more agile than companies that rigidly maintain the top-down approach.

The groundswell of the bottom-up way of adopting social tools inside the agile business keeps companies at the forefront of competitive information and gives them the ability to move quickly if the business needs to.

There are various catch-all names for social applications inside the firewall, from collaboration tools to contact managers, portals to productivity applications. Having information about your users embedded within these applications enhances the user experience and makes the collaboration site more engaging. Document versioning keeps track of multi-user edits, wikis provide up-to-date web pages and data points, and a good enterprise search solution keeps data alive. There are inbox rules to control the messages that flow into your mailbox, alerts to control changes to your documents, and status changes to control who can view your online presence; there are also ways to harness social computing tools. Using collaborative software will make your work inside the firewall more productive and effective, and users will not feel restricted. Capturing those chats around the coffee machine and harnessing them appropriately can spark the next business advantage you otherwise may have missed. You can transform your dated intranet to something that teams actually want to use.

Using the internal web
Intranets have been around for a while. They are generally searchable. They are repositories of data that contain historical documentation, facts and perhaps an organisation-wide telephone directory. Occasionally there may be a web page that contains news articles, social events and items to sell.

But there's so much more you can do with an intranet. Think of how you could improve it if you had a social computing platform for collaboration and customised it well. NASA is developing an intranet site called Spacebook.[50] The site will be useful for staff wanting to find out what's going on and engage with their colleagues, with real-time status updates, announcements and people search.

Sites like these appear to have all of the prerequisites for an engaging site. Staff need the ability to search for people and groups with similar skills, interests and job functions; the ability to capture status updates from colleagues on your friend list; the ability to add meta-information to documents so that popular documents about the topics you care about bubble up to the top of the intranet page. Furthermore, information about where your colleagues are right now means you can directly connect and interact with others in the team, group or organisation.

Keeping your data alive
Having a clear, simple to use site that is engaging and updated regularly is key to successful engagement inside the firewall. Collaboration suites such as Lotus Notes and Microsoft SharePoint are frameworks that can be installed out of the box to give a simple collaboration site, or they can be extensively customised with add-ons and scripting. This customisation provides the collaborative and engaging environment that your business requires and can, with the appropriate add-on software packages, turn an out of the box product into something that even NASA could be proud of. That can be the key to successful collaboration. If you build an effective interactive engagement network you will ensure that your staff will visit the site. The intranet site contains fresh and updated data and employees will regularly want to return to the site for their information. This keeps your data alive and turns the information into a strategic asset for the business, not terabytes of dead data taking up storage space in your data centre.

CUSTOMER SERVICE

Twitter helps turn around negative attitudes to products in almost real time – as the attitudes are actually forming amongst your audience. There are some superb examples of this effect. I've been really impressed with the way that companies use Twitter to connect with their customers. A friend of mine, Andrew, told me about his own personal experience of excellent and speedy service results through an initial conversation over Twitter.

Andrew and I both have a really slow broadband connection. We each get about 0.5 Mbps. So any calls that we make using Voice over IP (VOIP) can sometimes be a bit tortuous with the latency that we have to endure. The quality reminds me of my days in the Merchant Navy, using the VHF radio and speaking simplex commands like 'roger', 'over' and 'over and out'. The latency, especially using shared bandwidth after school hours, is sometimes very bad. Andrew complained about the speed of his broadband service to one of his contacts on Twitter:

> @raybooysen BT broadband running at 0.5 mbps (paying for 8) ,
> no BT Vision or XBVox live for me sob!
>
> *9:11 AM May 29th from TweetDeck in reply to raybooysen*

BT obviously monitors mentions of its name on Twitter using the search feature in its Twitter client and it responded within an hour of Andrew's original tweet.

> @raybooysen super impressed with BT they have already been
> onto me after the tweet
>
> *10:01 AM May 29th from TweetDeck in reply to raybooysen*

BT and Andrew had a few private conversations which were not visible on the main Twitter feed, so after a few tweets on Friday morning and a BT visit on Tuesday evening, Andrew was happy to report:

> BT improved my,broadband to 2.4 Mbps from 0.5 with a simple bit
> of rewiring and a dedicated faceplate, thanks guys
>
> *7:24 AM Jun 3rd from TweetDeck*

Which brought a response from BT:

BTCare: @**DeepFat** That's great news. Glad to hear it!
6 days ago from *web* · Reply · View Tweet

Andrew told me that BT even came down to his house a few days after this tweet to check the connections in the road in his village. BT demonstrated an excellent response to its customer issues, and all of this was initiated over Twitter.

Companies could certainly learn from this type of positive customer service and response using Twitter. This is just one example of how Twitter can be put to good use to change perception and improve satisfaction of a service, product or company amongst its customers. Credit should go to BT for being so responsive and getting great customer satisfaction from just one Tweet. Just think what this could do for your customers' perception of you.

Other companies use Twitter as a way of effectively engaging with their audience to track sentiment after an event. Selfridges in the UK is an example of this, responding to one of my own Twitter comments within 2 hours of my initial broadcast about an event I'd attended, see Figure 10.1.

Figure 10.1 Example of a brand monitoring customer comments

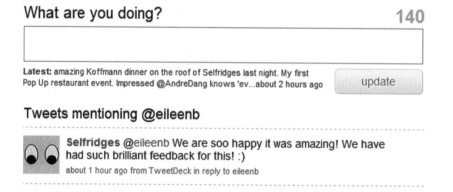

Customer service isn't all about customer complaints and giving the customer actual service. It's the customer connection, customer communication and customer engagement that make for good customer experience and ultimately a good perception of customer service.

The phenomenal popularity of a service like Twitter does bring its own challenges. People with a cause or a grievance will want to air it on the widest possible platform, and with sites like Twitter being watched and searched by millions, naturally these sites are a prime target.

Creating a plan if things go wrong

In the early days of Twitter, users used to complain about the 'fail whale'. This is the image that appears on Twitter's website whenever Twitter is over capacity and struggling to keep up with demand. In August 2009 there were several incidents where both Facebook and Twitter seemed to suffer from denial of service attacks which slowed the site down considerably and prevented users logging in. This caused an outcry as users struggled to access their favourite sites. Similar attacks occurred on LiveJournal, Blogger and YouTube which appeared to be co-ordinated attacks to prevent a prominent blogger from the Republic of Georgia from having any of his messages read by the media. Complaints from outraged users about Twitter and Facebook access became news. In December of the same year, a denial of service attack redirected the Twitter home page to a new screen alleging that the site had been 'hacked by Iranian Cyber Army' [sic]. Unfortunately these attacks pose a challenge for business. With increasing corporate and private user dependence on these types of sites, the potential for business disruption also increases if the sites are unavailable. These sites, which are out of your control, could be down for planned maintenance or they could become unavailable due to network issues or even subject to cyber attack from hackers.

> When you are planning your influencer strategy using freely available tools, you need to consider the impact if an attack like this happened. What would it mean for your business and for your customer satisfaction? You will need to devise an alternative plan to allow for situations of this kind.

With our plans in place we'll now start to really work the crowd. Let's use the platforms to market our products and generate some fans and let the information flow on in. (Oh, we'd better learn how to manage it too!)

SUMMARY

- Plan your collaboration strategy to avoid information islands and data silos.
- Find your noisy few to tell the story on your behalf.
- Teenage interaction on social networking sites is completely different than that of adults.
- Consider video sharing, podcasting and photo sharing in your channel planning.
- Use collaboration software for the exchange of intellectual capital inside the company.
- Enterprise search keeps data alive.
- Use tools like Twitter to enhance your customer service experience.
- Create a contingency plan in case the tools fail.

11 RELATIONSHIPS AND ENGAGEMENT

No, this is not the start of a soppy story about me. This chapter focuses on how to turn your casual friends into long lasting enthusiasts and advocates for your brand. We start off with a closer look at one of the most popular social networking tools for news propagation and general interaction – Twitter. We look at how Twitter has evolved and been changed by the actions of the its users, and how Twitter itself is changing how the media operates. We'll talk about how to recognise your advocates and consider the advantages of creating brand personalities who can carry the conversation on your behalf if you give them the correct information.

Next we'll have a look at how this new way of connecting to your customers has changed the way companies market their products by introducing a dynamic engagement model to their traditional marketing approach. Getting the correct strategy in place is very important as the two mechanisms complement each other and both need to work together in order to ensure success. We'll have a look at the sort of metrics you can consider when trying to measure your ROI and consider how to effectively capture the new two-way conversation with customers. Finally, we'll look at how to cope with the huge amounts of information coming at you, and consider ways of managing the information and using it to your advantage.

TWITTER FOR YOUR BUSINESS

Twitter has exploded in popularity since it was launched in 2006, and many businesses are capitalising on the real-time news feed by using it as a news broadcasting, customer service and information tool. Twitter is a microblogging service, where users post short 140 character status messages which are read by their followers. It has over 105 million registered users, and 300,000 new accounts are being created every day. Tweets can be responded to in several ways. You can send a reply that can be seen publicly, you can reply privately with a direct message, or you can forward a message to others using the retweet feature so that others can view your posts. You can use Twitter to talk about anything – from what you had for lunch to the government's latest budget cuts.

> On Twitter you can have an audience for whatever you wish to talk about.

It doesn't matter whether what you talk about is life changing or trivial – there is an audience for everything. Businesses are already capitalising on this viral effect.

There are hundreds of Twitter tips and tricks, Twitter do's Twitter don'ts and Twitter get rich quick schemes, but which one actually works? To fully understand the Twitter phenomenon and how to capitalise on it effectively, it's important to understand the fundamentals of how it works and why it's so successful. Is Twitter a broadcast medium, or something used for social conversations? Is it a feedback loop for customers or is it an advertising channel for marketers? Or is it actually all of these? The social media revolution isn't changing the way we use media, Twitter is changing the way we use media, and social networking has to move to accommodate these changes. Twitter has evolved since its inception because of the behaviour of its users. There is no definitive statement on the Twitter website about what it was supposed to be used for.

Twitter is a mechanism to communicate, connect and stay connected with online friends and co-workers through quick status updates.

Initially there was no standard way on Twitter to reply or to track interesting conversations on a given topic. The @ reply and the # hashtag were created by the Twitter community itself, which meant that conversation threads developed and communities evolved along similar interests. We wouldn't have become aware of the amount of news about the #iranelection, #swine_flu or #followfriday if these hashtags hadn't evolved and been used by the community. Of course, other hashtags had to evolve such as #fail and #misinformation to counter claims and criticisms on Twitter that turned out to be disappointing or untrue.

Making money from Twitter
There are over 15,000 registered Twitter applications, which represent a huge growth in popularity for Twitter.

Some of these applications aim to monetise Twitter by offering services so you can grow your Twitter followers, make money from click-throughs or analyse the friends and habits of the people who follow you.

If you have a good idea of your customers' desires and wants then you can target your marketing to more effectively connect with them. The majority of Twitter traffic (over 75% of traffic occurs outside Twitter.com) comes from third party Twitter clients and applications, with new clients appearing regularly. Regular Twitter users talk about the availability of the new Twitter client and their friends quickly adopt it if it suits them. Application designers are aware of this and adapt their software to suit this ever changing mode of interaction.

Twitter itself hasn't yet announced a formal advertising model to bring revenue to the start-up business, but it has announced a new advertising platform called 'Promoted Tweets' in April 2010. Promoted Tweets give companies the opportunity to pay for keywords and initialise a tweet in response. Future opportunities might include the opportunity to take advantage of geolocation so that companies with local branches can take advantage of the location to initialise local offers.

With over 19 billion search queries per month, the opportunity for Twitter to make money is huge. However, the value of Twitter as a social engagement tool seems to have reached the mature stage of the application life cycle model. The challenge for Twitter is that, with maturity, innovation has to occur to keep the service valuable and relevant and prevent users from abandoning the service for the next new thing.

Other businesses seem to be slower to take advantage of the marketing opportunity and people power of the word of mouth network. Some corporate teams already use Twitter to effectively gauge the pulse of their audience by evaluating comments and reactions. They support their audience, engage in dialogue, and they benefit from this new engagement with their customers. This online conversation seems to encourage better interaction and dialogue than blogs or forums. Whilst over 40% of Internet users have read a blog at some time or another, only about 5% of users blog on a daily basis. The simplicity of posting a Twitter update means that active Twitter contributors post frequently about things that might not make it into a blog post.

Hype or reality?

Let's be realistic about this, though. Most of us have never tweeted, nor have we ever read a tweet using a Twitter client. We might have heard about Twitter from the newspapers or the radio, but we are certainly not 'active' Twitter users

> Almost 90% of the content is produced by only 10% of Twitter users.

This is quite a lot different from numbers reported on other social networking sites, where 10% of users produce about 30% of the content. On Twitter, the average number of tweets produced per user is 1! Most of us will visit Twitter, we might create a profile and we might even broadcast a tweet. But that's all we will do, we won't tend to interact further and discover the value of Twitter. There are followers in Twitter who are consumers of information, they don't post content or updates, but they use Twitter as their source of information. They gather information without needing to post anything.

Marketing companies offer to get your message out to a much wider audience and in some cases can prove that your chosen Twitter phrase or word is becoming a trending topic for your campaign. However, these updates often seem to come from a set of 'fake accounts' with no information about the user, there is no interaction or dialogue with any of their followers. These 'buzz generation' accounts are published from a Twitter client like Seesmic or Hootsuite that has the ability to post from multiple different Twitter accounts at the same time. In reality, these fake accounts hold little value for either the feed consumer or the company commissioning the campaign and have no longevity in an ongoing marketing strategy.

So Twitter propagates information from a relatively small number of key influencers to the rest of us. These news instigators collate information and disseminate it to their loyal followers who then repost and retweet it to the rest of the Twitterari. This lack of structure and control is changing the way we look at digital media. Traditional marketing and digital media ran campaigns to drive our actions, whether that was clicking on a link, entering a competition or responding to a query. What we do now is changing the way we interact, and traditional media also needs to evolve from its traditional push marketing to conversational marketing. This approach, which has been driven by the interactivity of networking sites, is changing the nature of media messaging. Content is now free to be distributed in any way possible – by anyone with an online account and a device – and this has completely shifted power to the consumer. Everyone now has an opportunity to communicate across many channels. This gives everyone the opportunity to communicate, not necessarily to broadcast, with a select group of friends who can connect with **their** friends and pass the message on.

CULTIVATING YOUR ADVOCATES

When you have an online presence, it stands to reason that people are going to talk about your product, and it makes sense to connect with your customers by joining in the conversation. If you're a part of the conversation, then you have a great opportunity to influence that conversation, change perceptions and to create new advocates for your brand. But how can you scale your activities so that you connect with your audience and encourage **them** to connect with their networks? You need a plan. Your plan and activities must be structured to include everyone in the company who plans to connect with their audience. You need some guidelines.

CONNECTING WITH THE AUDIENCE

- You've recognised that your digital marketing and engagement approaches complement but do not replace your traditional methods of marketing. Traditional marketing is a timed, well controlled message delivered in a push campaign via various mechanisms and tracked via click-throughs, offer uptake and positive press reports.

- Your plan is to adopt some form of digital conversation and to bring a two-way dialogue into your marketing efforts and involve the voice of the customer. The new marketing is not about direct push any more, it's not about a two-way conversation.

- Take advice from others who have succeeded in this space. Successful companies who use these social tools listen first and sell second. In general, they act like aggregators and content providers rather than traditional advertisers, breaking the traditional marketing model.

- New media marketing provides valuable feedback about the brand whilst raising awareness about the brand offering. If the product is in beta, then this feedback loop can often drive the design of finished product which is more attractive to the consumer when the product launches.

Another advantage of using this type of customer engagement to market your brand is authenticity. Consumers value the interaction with the company, whether it's with you as a person, your team, or the organisation more broadly. The value is gained by having the direct connections with the consumer. In traditional marketing, this role is generally fulfilled by the PR spokesperson, someone who has been briefed in corporate messaging and ensures that the correct brand image is communicated. With these types of tools, everyone becomes a spokesperson. Anything you say on networking platforms can be perceived as being the 'official company line' so everyone with a public persona or online brand must be cognisant of corporate guidelines for social media and follow the corporate code of conduct.

Dealing with your company celebrities

Another thing to be aware of is that, by the very nature of this type of communicating, some of the personalities in your company may bubble up to the top of the pile and become individual celebrities due to their activities using social media tools and the perception of their influence by the community. These 'celebrities' can be used to your benefit. They can become your unofficial spokespeople for the company. This can lead to a positive impression for your brand as interest in the personality increases awareness of new features and news.

> Customers can then connect their perception of your brand to a real human being and not a logo.

Think about brands that with personalities at the helm: Victor Kiam and Remington, Steve Jobs and Apple, James Dyson and Dyson vacuum cleaners, Donatella Versace and the Versace fashion house. These leaders are all great personalities; they are spokespeople and living embodiments of the brand. Glossy magazines, offering a glimpse into celebrities' lives, bring awareness of the celebrity, and, by extension, their product, book or film, by this human connection.

The same is true for celebrities who use social media. Sarah Brown, the wife of the former UK prime minister, and Barack Obama use Twitter as a way as connecting to their audience. Ashton Kutcher has almost 6 million Twitter followers, Oprah Winfrey has over 4 million and Stephen Fry almost 2 million. Each of these personalities has brought this connection off the pages of the glossy magazines and into the online world of interactivity.

> The empathy that your social media spokespeople develop with your customers brings a much closer connection to the customer. The bond created with the brand evangelist becomes close and personal, and, by extension, the bond to the brand which can lead to loyalty and advocacy in future.

If you are trying to increase your social media advocates, perhaps consider the following activities to help drive engagement:

DRIVING CUSTOMER ENGAGEMENT

- Build demand. Information fuels itself. Drive the thirst for knowledge amongst your audience and keep them engaged with information that they would find difficult to find externally.

- Drive awareness. Make sure that the consumers are kept up to date about your products. In their day job, they may not have time to discover everything about your product set. Tell them about it, and reinforce the message regularly. Ask the audience questions, interact and inform.

- Show the new. In technology, consumers want to see your product vision and direction. When a product is ready to talk about, encourage your teams to talk about it, show video clips, images and demos. Get the word out and spread the buzz.

- Show value. If used correctly, social media can demonstrate the value to customers after they have purchased your product. Whether this is ongoing support, customer care, interaction, help and dialogue, the connection is there and should be encouraged to develop.

To preserve your brand and maintain its visibility in the markets, it is important to maintain a good ongoing connection with your customers. There are several ways to do this, but Dell certainly shows leadership with several innovative ideas. In addition to their financially successful Twitter aliases, Dell has other community innovations.

Dell have created a micro-site called IdeaStorm which encourages comments, good and bad, about Dell's products.

This enables users to be in direct touch with Dell about the issues that are important, such as customer service, pre and post sales processes and product quality. The rationale behind this idea is that it is better to allow customers to complain and rant about problems directly to Dell, than have detractors complain on other sites where the comments are harder to find and subsequently fix. Sites like these don't stop customers complaining on other sites, but do allow the complaints to be heard by Dell itself; and by listening to their customers, they also gather ideas for future products.

SOCIAL MARKETING

There are myriad social media, social networking, social computing and social business sites on the web, all of them encouraging conversations with millions of people who use various mechanisms to connect, communicate and collaborate through a variety of channels. Traditional marketing campaigns now have to have a digital component to ensure that they are reaching the correct segment of the audience, and there are lots of case studies about success and positive ROI from web campaigns.

But can social marketing be measured at all? How do you measure your ROI? It's very simple to measure ROI through traditional channels such as printed media, radio or TV advertising. There are methods of measuring ROI from search marketing also – via click-throughs from a web page. Social marketing often isn't measured directly, although there are several tools that you can use to measure how many customers have clicked on your links. Interesting and useful content is transmitted virally, through recommendations, word of mouth, email and link forwarding.

> If you try to sell directly to the customer using social marketing, you might be disappointed.

Tweeting about the same links over and over again or pushing the same message on your Facebook page will drive customers away. You need to think of your online strategy in a different way. Different rules apply to social marketing than in other, more traditional forms of marketing.

But ROI is a very difficult thing to measure through something as intangible as a social media campaign, a blogging strategy or web competition. Case studies are examples of success in the corporate world, and they are also a key indicator of sentiment and success in the social media space.

Old Spice had an innovative way to persuade women to buy Old Spice in the US. They launched an online video campaign called 'the man your man can smell like'. The campaign was launched during Superbowl week and targeted TV programmes where viewers would likely watch together. In the first three months of 2010, mentions of the Old Spice brand captured 75% of all conversations, with half of the conversations initiated by women. Other videos started to appear parodying the Old Spice advert and style of conversation, and TV presenters like Oprah mentioned the brand on her show.

The agency then hit upon a great way to capture the real-time messages on Facebook, Twitter and YouTube.

> The Old Spice response campaign became the fastest growing campaign ever, reaching 5.9 million views on YouTube on day 1.

On day 2, Old Spice was mentioned in 8 out of the top 11 most popular videos on the web. On day 3 of the campaign there were more than 20 million views, and on day 7 over 40 million. This had a huge knock-on effect on the Old Spice Twitter and Facebook pages. The Old Spice website had a 300% increase in site visits and became the most popular channel on YouTube. Financially this campaign has made a difference too, with sales of Old Spice body wash up by 27% in 6 months since campaign launch. A great return on investment from a TV and YouTube video campaign.

Businesses need to take advantage of the engagement with the consumer, capturing stories and success measures from their online population, and they need to engage with their key customers and encourage their online influencers to become champions for the brand. Some companies toy with the idea of social media, and consider using it to further their market in order to gain a deeper understanding of their audience and improve perceptions, interaction and feedback. However, there are lots of differing opinions on what constitutes an effective social media strategy, without any clear consensus on which is the best way forward. One size does not fit all. Your strategy should suit your company and it should work for your business. There are, as yet, no clearly defined standards for social marketing.

Objective based social marketing campaigns

There are lots of email campaign software packages which will help you track email click-throughs to help you become more effective in determining which parts of your content are successful. It is important to understand what is relevant and important to your audience so you can track key market trends – what is hot at the moment and what is not in your market. Analysing your metrics and performance helps you to get as much data as possible from any analysis tools that you use. It is much more difficult to measure the ROI from social marketing than from traditional marketing, and that's why measuring the effectiveness of any online marketing activities you do is vital to your go-to-market strategy.

There are three basic rules for social media if you think of it in terms of marketing:

- Influence is everything. Strive to influence positive responses from your audience.
- Engage the audience and engender open discussions.
- Use these positive responses and open discussions to develop your online relationship with your consumer.

Your objectives need to be clearly defined from the outset. This approach is often not about the direct sale to the customer, although Dell has managed to use offers delivered through Twitter to achieve direct sales with its DellOutlet Twitter account. Are your current online efforts making the impact you want them to in the market? Are they having any impact at all? If you haven't defined your objectives and end goals clearly enough then your business leaders will be quickly disappointed by the end result, and your investment in time and money will be wasted if your senior leaders come to the conclusion that your approach has no value or is of no help to the company's bottom line.

Bacardi in Ireland has had success in engaging its audience through Facebook. Its distributors switched from micro-sites to a Facebook page in 2008 and created an application within Facebook for any competitions it would run. Its campaigns focus on user interaction and it encourages comments on each of its Facebook entries. It also engages the users, responds to comments quickly and grows its fan base by asking people to 'like' its Facebook page in order to enter the competition. This is a successful strategy which gives Bacardi great engagement and interaction.

Before you embark on the measurement of metrics it's important to consider the costs of this strategy, which is not only a financial cost to the business, but is also the time that you and your staff have invested in using the tools to promote your brand or product. If you're hosting your own company blogs, then you need to consider the cost of bandwidth, blogging software and server power to cope with the increased traffic your success will bring. When Twitter started out, every tweet sent by every user was in the software, housed on a couple of servers under a desk in the office in California. As more and more people used the network in the early days, it was plagued by downtime and an over capacity message accompanying an image of birds trying to hold a whale aloft – an image that early Twitter users quickly termed the 'fail whale'.

> You need to consider how you would deal with runaway success in carrying out your social media strategy.

You may have created the next darling of the social media world – the next Twitter for example so you need to account for the possibility that this could happen when you create social media strategy and plan. You also need to consider whether the ROI actually is more than the amount you've invested to implement your strategy.

When considering your strategy, you will be faced with a huge number of options and tools that you can use. Try not to use the scatter gun approach and 'launch' in every area you can. Filter out the tools that will not be valuable to you. Should you consider Bebo, which is primarily used by younger users, for example, if you work for a heavy engineering company and want to market tooling?

Use a rating scale for these tools and decide which of your chosen channels will be valuable to you. Grade them on, say, a nine-point scale to make sure you choose the most appropriate for your business. Have a look at your own business and decide whether a social media strategy would be appropriate, or which parts of your business would benefit from using social media to broadcast your message. There are some factors which may negatively impact perception of your brand online and other opportunities to enhance your brand. Try using a SWOT (strengths, weaknesses, opportunities and threats) analysis – just as you would when pursuing a large business deal, to see whether you actually want to go forward with the plan at all.

DEALING WITH THE FLOOD OF INFORMATION

You can easily become overwhelmed when you try to stem the flow of information from the 'fire hose', and might consider having only one 'corporate' presence on the web. There are great advantages to having corporate level social destinations, such as DellOutlet, MarksandSpencer and Google, who are a credible voice for interacting with the consumer, and a great push news channel for the company. But this often detracts from the benefits gained from the interaction with the 'human voice' of the company. These social destinations can play a key proactive role in producing major announcements and could be considered as part of an overall social media marketing plan. Having a centralised blog or Twitter feed makes it easy for consumers to check news when information gets out to the web, but this does have the potential to become just another sanitised news feed for the PR team – which detracts from the concept of direct engagement with the customer.

The chief marketing officer of Novell, John Dragoon, has his own blog and is also a key contributor to the Novell News blog. With eight other contributors, this blog is a single place to go to for news and opinions across the company from senior leaders. This doesn't seem to be a new PR initiative as John has been blogging for 4 years now and also occasionally updates his Twitter stream. Carefully managed, this approach can work well.

Blogs from company bloggers could be aggregated into one centralised RSS feed so that journalists can follow the corporate master feed. Mary Jo Foley, who has followed Microsoft for over 20 years, follows the main feed from every blogger in the company. She uses Google Reader to categorise the news makers, the key influencers and the interesting people, and scans through the rest of the feed when she has the time.

There is also the option to use an RSS feed to populate a master corporate Twitter feed which customers can follow too. My gut feeling is that this feed would need to be filtered so that duplicate information was removed, and irrelevant posts excluded. This would take a large investment of time for larger companies which would need to fully understand every product, brand and marketing strategy across the whole company, and it would be a huge undertaking for the team involved. I feel this would take away the personality from the interaction with the customer – moving this closer to a PR message than the voice of the individual influencer.

> With the huge variety of channels to communicate through, and the vast amount of information flowing through each channel, the potential to become overwhelmed can be huge.

It's therefore a good idea to get teams working together and contributing to the channel, which can give a balanced perspective to the feed and introduce individual personalities to communications. To track who is communicating on a channel such as Twitter, tools like Co-Tweet, TweetFunnel and HootSuite have the facility to have multiple authors contributing to the feed and allow the user name to be appended to the outbound message.

Applying filters is another good idea to manage the flow. Grouping search results enables you to track campaigns and customer queries. Analytics tools can track sentiment and guide you towards areas that you need to focus on first. If you are aware of the amount of information you need to work through then you can manage the flow appropriately with the correct tools and measurements.

Our social media strategy is going well. We're on track to be successful, but we're struggling with how we can scale. Now let's let the crowd work for **us** and get them to amplify our message.

- Use Twitter to connect with your customers and engage them in dialogue.
- Listen first and sell second.
- Case studies are a key indicator of success and sentiment.
- Encourage your online influencers to become your brand champions.
- Use filters to reduce the amount of information you receive and make sure you only see the kinds of information that are relevant to your business.

12 AMPLIFYING YOUR MESSAGE

Communities aren't a new concept. Communities have existed in face to face interactions since humans lived in groups. It is still possible to create a brand new community from scratch if you need to. If you want to create a community specifically to enthuse about your new product, we'll see how to build a successful community by following a couple of rules. First, we will look at why influencers in the community are so important in sustaining the community and propagating messages. We will look at trust and how to harness the knowledge through the initiators and trusted advisers in the community. Secondly, we'll look at the different ways that buzz is created, starting with an initiator with an innovative idea that goes viral, and then we'll look at the way that large companies create communities. We'll see how the word of mouth network and the power of the people work together to amplify the message, and we'll look at how tools like Facebook have become the mechanism to amplify this message in minutes instead of days. We'll talk about network effects and how social causes take advantage of these effects to raise vast sums of money through the use of online games. We'll see whether placing news sites behind pay walls will reduce these network effects or sustain them, and we'll look at whether licensing deals are the preferred option for companies to access and expose data through search engines. Finally, we'll look at different ways of measuring reach for your social media activities. We'll see how different tools manage and assess social graph data, sentiment and metrics, and consider how lead generation can be measured using social media alongside your normal sales process in the company.

COMMUNITIES AND INFLUENCERS

Communities exist wherever you look, both inside and outside business. There are groups of like-minded people who come together for a short time to support a good cause. There are groups of people who spend time helping others in user forums. There are communities that share news articles of interest and links to interesting topics. There are also people who are dedicated to helping to increase the store of knowledge on the Internet by creating articles on Wikipedia. These people don't expect rewards for their actions.

Their desire to help others is driven by nothing more than just that – a desire to help.

There are a large number of people out there who want to help you achieve your goals, and if you want to build a community you can turn this desire to your advantage. All you need to do is find **the correct people in the community** and channelling it correctly.

Communities are formed when people come together to share knowledge, ideas and support each other in a self sustaining group. Communities tend to have three basic behaviour characteristics:

- **Advocacy.** Members of the community are evangelists for their group and recommend products and services to other members and groups.
- **Connectedness.** Community members have connections to other experts in the industry – or they know who to contact when additional help is needed.
- **Reputation.** Members of the community are recognised experts in their area, they have been discovered for their skills and ability, and they have a good reputation and often a great reach across their sphere of influence.

Without these characteristics, communities often fragment and fade. The simplicity of successful communities often comes down a matter of basic trust. Community members trust other members within the group itself, and they trust other community members for their skills and knowledge within the group. The community, although often appearing to be disorganised and chaotic, actually works in an organic and simplistic way. The weak ties within the community connect with the stronger ties and glue the group together. Unfortunately, as communities grow in size, usually organically, people tend to try to impose some type of order and rules on the group.

Placing mandates, edicts or over-stringent regulations onto communities can create factions and discord within the community itself.

Sometimes the community may fragment and create spinoff groups who may work against the main community itself. These 'special interest groups' are useful in some ways. For example, you might have a suite of products with a strong following (like Apple has). Apple might wish to encourage the special interest groups that form for the iPad to become completely different groups than those formed for the iPhone.

Segmenting groups into special interest groups can vastly increase the size of each community, whilst maintaining a consistent messaging framework across the product suite.

There's a great deal of knowledge within a community that can be harnessed if you wish. Knowledge can be spread really effectively if you can find your community initiators and use their knowledge and desire to help you.

An initiator is someone – perhaps a group – with a real passion for their subject.

Furthermore, your initiators will have a desire to broadcast interesting material. These initiators may have created their own area on the web, often a website or blog, which is filled with information and often stored purely for their own interest. They will have collected as much information as they can, store it on the web and add to the store whenever they get new snippets of information. With search technologies and web crawlers the site will become visible to others and more and more people will become aware of the knowledge repository on the site.

If the site has Web 2.0 features embedded which allow comments then users will start to contribute and interact, and the community will start to grow.

Some hobby sites have come to the attention of corporations which acquire them in order to add to their advertising revenue stream. The Pistonheads forum in the UK, which is a place for car enthusiasts, is a good example of a hobby site which has come to the attention of the media.

Creating a community

If you want to create a community from scratch and don't currently know who your community initiator could be, then you might like to think about a new and oblique approach to community-generating activities.

GENERATING COMMUNITY

- For example, you might have a website with a new community upload photo stream that you'd like to draw users' attention to. You could approach various photographic hobbyist sites or clubs, perhaps to encourage a photography competition. You could then have the results shown on your website. This would bring new visitors to your website from the hobby site who may not have been aware of it before.

- You might have a new product that you'd like to test on a different set of users who are not participating in formal beta downloads of technical support forums. One of your approaches could be to target other communities. You could include communities who are advocates for similar or competing products to yours and you could start to engage with them on a regular basis. You may not be able to convert them to become product evangelists for your new product, but you will be able to tap into a community with an existing voice.

- You can try to use a new stream of advertising to find your new community volunteers. You could ask questions in existing communities like 'Would you like to become part of a customer panel or an opinion panel?' or 'Would you like to road-test some new products?' You could watch the responses, both positive and negative, and see who appears to be the influencer in the community. Your initiators will often respond to your initial query in order to further their search for more knowledge.

You may not find your ideal initiator right at the start as the embryonic community emerges. If you give the community time, it will evolve organically and your new community initiators will drive the community forward for you.

Community buzz

There are many different ways to create buzz about your product or brand. The challenge for a lot of businesses is that they may not have the benefit of a large corporation like Google or Kraft Foods behind them. However, with the word of mouth network, individuals can sometimes create enough buzz on their own to sway a whole industry. It's quite interesting to realise that the major industries and corporations don't always have the largest voice when buzz is created through use of the network and tools.

The voice of the community can often drown out the official message from the company.

Sometimes one person alone can have enough influence amongst his peers and connections to create significant buzz through his social network and his friends of friends network.

An example occurred on Facebook over a period of 2 weeks in December 2009. In the run-up to Christmas every year there is a battle for supremacy in the music industry. Each music company wants its Christmas song to make it to the top of the music charts. For several years now, the reality TV show, X Factor, has achieved this in the UK. The winner of the TV talent competition is more or less guaranteed chart success. Simon Cowell, who has great influence in the music industry, is one of the judges and also owns the rights to the TV show.

When it became apparent that again, for the fifth year running, the Christmas number one record was going to be the winner of X factor, Jon and Tracy Morter, from Essex in the UK, decided to protest. The Morters used Facebook to create a group dedicated to trying to stop the winner of the X Factor competition from reaching in the top of the charts. They wanted a music group called Rage against the Machine to get to number one instead. This seemed an impossible task. The X Factor winner in 2009, Joe McElderry, looked certain to rise to the top of the charts. What the Morters tried to do was to encourage users through Facebook to buy a different record.

Rage against the Machine is a punk band from the US who had released a single which was not expected to do very well in the UK charts. However, Rage against the Machine did have an advantage over Joe McElderry. Their single was only available to purchase as a download from the web. Unfortunately Joe McElderry's marketing team either didn't want or had forgotten to make this purchasing method available from the start. This omission gave Rage against the Machine a huge advantage.

The Facebook group grew to over 700,000 fans in a very short time. There were 200,000 fans on a backup Facebook page and over 500,000 fans on the main

Facebook page. Both pages had the same message and the instructions were really simple. The tactic was to simply buy a copy of the Rage against the Machine single online within a limited time window. So from 13 to 20 December 2009, every member of each dedicated Facebook group was encouraged to purchase one copy of the single from the web. The simplicity of Facebook and the friends of friends system meant that all members of the Facebook page were encouraged to pass on the message and to persuade others in their networks to buy the downloaded single too. This simple method worked very well indeed.

Rage against the Machine reached number one in the UK charts on 20 December. The band were completely unprepared for their massive and unexpected success in the UK and have promised to do a free gig in the UK in 2010 as a thank-you for all the support from Facebook fans. Simon Cowell was gracious in defeat. He called Jon Morter to congratulate him on his Facebook campaign. This upset made the news everywhere. Jon found himself thrust into the limelight both in the UK and in the US, giving interviews in both countries explaining why he did this. This simple effect proves that people power effectively transcends geographical boundaries when a campaign is done well.

This demonstrates just how significant the word of mouth network is. It demonstrates the power of connections. Friends who connect with each other can share information and create enough buzz to have a greater network effect than traditional push. This particular collaborative effort has been achieved without the huge amounts of work that would have been needed in the past in order to rally a huge group like this.

Facebook has become the mobilisation tool of the 21st century.

When groundswell happens like this, it proves that the ordinary person, the man on the street, does have an influence and does have a voice after all.

Together with the power of connections and crowd sourcing, it's a rather powerful voice – as Facebook has proved over and over again...

VIRAL AWARENESS

If you want success, it's a good idea to think about network effects. People tend to congregate where their friends are, they buy what their friends recommend and they use the products that their friends use. This effect is known as the **cluster effect**, and social network applications need to be designed with these clusters in mind.

In early January 2010, when most of the news channels were reporting how the UK was paralysed under a blanket of snow, a ripple effect started to occur on Facebook. Facebook started to display status updates containing only one word (or occasionally two): 'lemon', 'nude', 'black', 'tartan', 'dirty grey'. These updates caused speculation amongst male users before word got out that this was all about underwear and the colour we were wearing that day. These status updates had a knock-on effect in raising awareness about breast cancer. Facebook groups dedicated to breast cancer awareness gathered over 40,000 fans supporting the cause, with some fans posting images of them wearing bras on the group pages. The Susan G. Komen for the Cure breast cancer foundation reported that, due to the Facebook status updates, their Facebook fans jumped in number from 134,000 to 154,000.[51] 'We're so delighted,' said spokeswoman Andrea Rader. 'We think this is just a phenomenal example of how powerful the Internet can be in getting this message out.'

Another example of a Facebook group being used to raise awareness and get help quickly was for Philip Pain, a student.[52] Philip fell from a seventh-floor balcony in Mazatlán, Mexico, crushing his internal organs and breaking his legs and back. The local hospital didn't have enough supplies of his rare blood type, O-negative, to operate and save his life. Less than 6% of the population have O-negative blood, so shortages can be expected. His parents set up a Facebook group asking for blood, and within hours 12 pints of blood were flown in from Florida. A further 8 pints were donated at the hospital in Mazatlán and other O-negative donors signed up to an emergency blood list ready to donate if needed. Facebook notified enough people so that there were sufficient supplies of blood available quickly, which meant that doctors were able to start the operation to save his life.

These are amazing examples of how individual voices can be magnified and used with the network effect in order to create a viral effect for good causes.

> Awareness grows about the cause, people become mobilised into action and you can reach millions of people by using a site like Facebook.

ONLINE GAMING FOR SOCIAL CAUSES

There are many opportunities for networking tools to be put to good use for social causes. These networks have become powerful in helping to raise money and awareness about social issues around the world. Zynga, one of the leading MMORPG developers has several social games on Facebook with a huge number of players. Their top games are Mafia Wars, Farmville, FishVille, CafeWorld and Zynga Poker. When the Haiti earthquake struck, Zynga responded very quickly to the need for international aid. It offered 'limited edition social goods' including 'non withering white corn within Farmville'. Farmville has over 75 million online users who can use real money to purchase Farmville vouchers and exchange them for high value items. Zynga also offered a 'Haitian drum on Mafia Wars' to its 23 million users and 'a special chip package' in Zynga Poker. They announced that they would donate 100% of the proceeds to support emergency aid in Haiti through its relief fund.[53] Previous efforts from Zynga in selling seeds for Haiti had earned over $1 million and the opportunity to buy virtual pets in YoVille raised $90,000 for the San Francisco Society for the Prevention of Cruelty to Animals.

Other initiatives allowed players to purchase virtual goods to aid the World Food Program.

Social media has benefited good causes many times. In addition to the great work done by Zynga, other social media channels have been used. Twit Cause asks for causes to be nominated and companies offer donations to the cause for each tweet recorded. Häagen-Dazs donated $1 for any tweet which referenced the hashtag #HelpHoneyBees. Other initiatives have included offering $24,000 for cancer research and donating money to keep teenagers off the streets.

> There are opportunities here to monetise your social media efforts in the third sector (Charities and not for profit organisations) and generate significant revenue if you can take advantage of network effects.

Facebook, MySpace and Bebo make money through targeted advertising on their home pages. Twitter, on the other hand, currently loses money as it doesn't yet have a strategy to earn revenue through click-through Twitter messages. However, several of Twitter's third party applications, analytics and sentiment trackers do have paid-for sustainable subscription models. Twitter itself has recently announced a revenue model for sponsored accounts and links which will advertise services and goods.

In order to create a popular site that will draw your users in for the first time and keep them coming back you need to be creative. Think about how you can turn your site into a business which keeps on generating revenue and increasing its online activities in the long term. This can be achieved through advertisements, membership fees, subscriptions or eBook downloads. The *Times* newspaper in the UK has now changed to a subscription model for its web content, which is now hidden behind a pay wall. This move is being closely monitored by other online newspapers to gauge its success and to determine whether other news sites will follow this model. Will every item of news ultimately be situated behind a pay wall? Where will this news be collected from? Will any of the news then get disseminated through social channels? It's difficult to predict at the moment. Wikipedia is determined to provide content for free for its readers. The site's founder, Jimmy Wales, asks for donations for the upkeep of the site through its Wikimedia Foundation and so far has managed to achieve his goals without resorting to paid for advertising.

> Monetisation and passive income generation need to be part of your strategy to make your sites financially sustainable in the long run.

It seems like licensing deals may be an answer to sites that need to think about continued revenue. Microsoft adopted the policy of licensing its software right from the start of its business, and this policy has continued to give it ongoing revenue year on year as new products are released. Perhaps your business also lends itself well to licensing of your content. There could then be opportunities to offer licensed access to the Twitter stream, your Twitter results will appear on search engine lists and you then have a viable option that will provide ongoing revenue for Twitter itself.

RECORDING AND TRACKING

In the normal course of business, sales leads are tracked for each customer pre-sales engagement and each deal closed is a success. This is also true of any leads that are generated from your digital marketing initiatives. You can track who follows you, or who clicks on your link and visits your website. You can see which site has generated the click-through. You can also see who has continued their journey through the site and which of these visitors actually turns into a valid business opportunity. If you know which social site has generated the most click-through opportunities then there is a great opportunity for you to increase engagement with your audience by increasing your communication on that particular site. Recording and tracking these metrics can give you enough information to create an easy to digest summary of your progress. The decision makers can see that your efforts have been fruitful with month on month growth, brand awareness and presence. This report then can be used to validate your investment in your social initiative.

The use of search facilities on blogs and on Twitter can highlight mentions of your brand name which can then be used to track the increase or decrease in the number of people talking about your brand or product. These statistics can be used to calculate month on month growth (or decline) in brand mentions. This can be automated by the use of alerts or by using a sentiment measuring tool to watch change in satisfaction with your brand.

So you now have all of the pieces in place for a successful strategy. You know how social engagement works and the tools you need to use. You know why you need a great presence and effective ways to create, manage and maintain a good online brand. You are happy with the perception of your brand and how to effectively manage your reputation. You've implemented policies to manage staff use of social tools guided by thought leaders in digital engagement. You know how to find your audience, listen to them and engage with the right influencers. You've taken advantage of the strong and weak ties in your network and explored ways to leverage your influencer network. You've reached out beyond your immediate network and gathered new connections. You have a great understanding about behaviour and scale and you have generated advocates for your brand. You've generated buzz, have a viral effect going from time to time so you can sit back and relax, right?

Wrong. With the speed of change in our always on, always connected, digital world, nothing is fixed in stone. Everything is fluid and changes with the speed of a mouse click.

You need to be ahead of the game for your business to be agile.

Your existing investment in time and money needs to produce results for the next few years, which is difficult in this rapidly changing environment. So how can you stay ahead of the curve and continue to be a thought leader in your business? Predicting the digital engagement trends of the future will help you be one step ahead of the competition.

So let's gaze into my crystal ball and have a go at predicting what sort of evolution we're going to see next and whether we'll need a brand new crowd to work with.

- Find the recognised experts in your area.
- Don't place mandates and rules on the community. It will fragment and separate.
- One well connected individual has the ability to create significant buzz in the community.
- Think about Facebook and its ability to share links for your business channel.
- Try to create something that will go viral.
- Social causes can benefit from online gaming. Think about opportunities to earn revenue for the third sector.
- Keep alert for the pace of change and watch for leading indicators.

13 WHERE IS IT ALL GOING?

In this, the final chapter, we take a look forward. We look at what will happen next in the new world of communication. Just as the dotcom boom changed the way we used the web in the late 1990s, so the influx of social media platforms will fundamentally change the way we communicate and do business in the 2010s. First, we'll have a look at the new way of marketing and how push marketing will have to evolve to suit the new dialogue. Secondly, we'll speculate on the new plat-form and how search will play an important part in raising awareness of social engagement tools and encourage more people to take part in the conversation. We'll have a look at how hardware will evolve to take the users to the next level of engagement and how the infrastructure will change to support our changing requirements on the web. We'll talk about the blurring of our work and social lives and the privacy and personas that we'll need to adopt online to keep our public and private lives separate. Finally, I'll share a few tips to help you become successful at engaging with the online audience without becoming overwhelmed in the crowd.

Forrester's Technographic ladder (http://bit.ly/bn6fDc) shows that consumers are collectors, critics, conversationalists and creators and that their engagement in-creases year on year.[54] There is a great opportunity to engage with the audience, have a two-way conversation and complement the traditional push marketing approach.

This engagement, carried out where the audience spend their online social hours, gives companies a great opportunity to generate brand advocacy and change perceptions and impact.

In order to achieve marketing success with engagement marketing using online social media, a long term strategy needs to be created. This new way of working is a long term commitment and a valuable business proposition, but it cannot happen on its own.

This approach takes time and effort to reap the appropriate rewards as each member of the team needs to contribute to and invest in the conversation.

Social media activities are not another push medium for marketers but used in a push–pull way to orchestrate engagement and dialogue with their tier 1 influencers. Regular engagement is necessary for sustained channel growth and there should be activity in each social media channel which can be measured as the conversational responses increase throughout the year.

I do have a word of warning, however, in this new world of marketing. Be cautious of relying on recording the volume of users, followers, fans and friends across each channel. This type of metrics monitoring will not bring any great insight to the business.

> Take time to develop your own insight into your audience. Work out an appropriate baseline to build upon, and think carefully about the use of any tools which automate responses as these will quickly damage perceptions of your brand.

Longevity is also important. Any commitment to these types of activities should be for a period one of at least a year to allow you to set a baseline and introduce effective monitoring and tracking. This allows appropriate themes to be created and dialogue with influencers to be developed throughout your audience.

THE NEW WAY OF USING THE PLATFORM

There has been a lot of speculation and head scratching about the next version of Facebook, the new Twitter or the next generation of social media platforms. Analysts, businesses and the community are all trying to predict what will dominate the market, and which product will be one step ahead when the new generation of tools appear. There are several conflicting schools of thought here. My own theory about what's going to happen is totally different from those of some of my technical colleagues in the industry, but it resonates well with what others say. The future depends on your point of view of course – on whether you view social media as an enterprise discussion or a consumer discussion. Both are valid points. However, the main methods that tie both of these enterprise and consumer markets together are mobility and search.

One of the biggest step changes we will see in social media is through the advancement of search. Search will play a powerful role in making new social media items discoverable. Currently search engines often display blog posts and forum comments, videos and podcasts. Google has already launched itself into the social space with its Google Buzz service. Real-time items in Buzz already display in Google search results. Facebook, traditionally a walled garden, now has items appearing on search pages and Google Alerts will show the latest tweets for your user name and where they have been syndicated.

As search engines strike further deals with social media application providers, information or status updates will be returned in search results outside the social media application itself. This is available at the moment, albeit in a limited functionality, but trending news items on Digg, trending topics on Twitter and widely shared items on Facebook could soon appear in search results for your query along with ordinary search results. The exposure of real-time results will have quite far reaching effects on the way we interact. This advancement will bring more people into engaging with social media sites.

People who don't traditionally class themselves as social media consumers or users will be exposed to new forms of media information through searches. This will enable new consumers to interact with each other and engage with your brand. Over time, this new way of interaction will permeate more into the way we use search with search engine enhancements. Perhaps there will be the ability to refine search results by your social group, which may encourage more social types of searches.

As bandwidth available to homes and mobile devices increases, the way we use video will change. Real-time video chat channels will empower the information worker to work more dynamically. This increase means that more and more of us can work from home and have a good video connection for face to face meetings with our colleagues in the office. Free or low cost WiFi will become more widespread and accessible, enabling mobile workers to remain connected wherever they are. TV and video on demand will provide access across many channels to deliver a consistent experience across PCs and mobile devices. Streaming video will be delivered directly to movie theatres so that within 10 years we will be able to see a high quality streamed movie on the day that it is released worldwide.

Applications like Facebook, which provide users with the ability to chat over instant messaging in real time, will dominate more traditional static applications. Switching from instant messages to video within the application will become simple. Social media applications will strive to become your universal inbox. Filtering systems will become more commonplace in applications as users seek to categorise their many different networks of friends and connections.

THE MOBILE OPPORTUNITY

Mobile devices will become the hub of social media communications, and operate at all levels of our connected lives. There will be an abundance of location aware applications providing useful information to connect users face to face who happen to be in the same location.

Consumers will drive the next evolution of social media applications for mobile devices and many applications will disappear as new technologies (such as GPS location aware applications) evolve.

Mobile phone manufacturers are creating applications for the phone, but there's a problem. There are currently no set standards for application development across mobile device platforms. If one user is using an iPhone and the other is using a Nokia, there are limited chances for interaction between the two devices. Applications which have been developed for different models of the Windows phone need to be modified to suit each different model. Users want technologies and applications for their mobile device but with the lack of cross-platform support in mobiles, it is difficult to get any cluster effects.

Without these cluster effects, the technology will not be widely adopted. Without wide adoption, there will be no impetus to develop new technologies. And with the huge amount of different devices that are available across different platforms, there are limited opportunities to move forward. So how do you get access to the same platform from all these different devices? The obvious solution is to develop your application to work on the browser. You would also need to make sure that all applications that have been written for the browser comply with international standards. This ensures that your application will work across all of the mobile device platforms and all of the different operating systems and hardware. Or you could buy an iPad...

In hardware terms, the Apple iPad will completely redefine the way we think about consumer devices and interaction on the web. Those that struggle with the form factor of the small smartphones or have chunky fingers will welcome this new device. Anyone who has problems interacting effectively with the tiny keypads will embrace this new form of communication. The iPad will drive greater consumer engagement, and social media will be the vehicle of communication. Augmented reality applications on the iPad will bring a new dimension to e-commerce.

Privacy will become more granular, as social media items become more discoverable. Profiles will be customisable for your different online personas. For example, you may want to customise different settings for your work persona compared with the settings for your home persona. Then there are the other roles you might have. You may be a school governor; you may sit on a committee or a council. You may perform charity work anonymously, or you may be a silent and invisible spectator. There will be new mechanisms in place on social platforms which will ensure that the setting you adopt to communicate with your friends will not cross boundaries into your corporate life.

Conversely, collaboration applications inside the firewall will evolve to incorporate social media connectors and features within the enterprise application.

The email client will become much more than just a place to receive email and view your calendar. Email will include threaded conversations, status updates from presence aware applications, video and instant messaging. Some of these features are already present in clients such as Outlook and Notes. You will be able to seamlessly switch between Facebook type applications and your inbox. Your Twitter stream and your RSS feeds will be accessed from one place. Your work life and your social life will blur. The application shift from your work life to your personal life will become more streamlined and transparent. Companies will adopt social software more readily as they realise that effective employee collaboration in whatever format makes for more productive working environments. There will be a grass roots adoption of social media platforms inside the firewall as an aid to communication and effective interaction.

But most of all, social media, in whatever form, is here to stay. Do you want to join in the great conversation or do you want to watch it happening? Whatever your choice is, I hope you will benefit from the newsmakers, the influencers and the huge amount of knowledge from the rest of the crowd.

SUMMARY

- Search and mobility will drive the future of social media.
- Location aware applications will present a great business opportunity for the developer.
- Collaboration inside the company will be connected to social software applications to pool knowledge and extend connections.
- Social media is not going to go away. Companies must change their plans to incorporate the new way of communicating to avoid being left behind in the marketplace.

NOTES

1. http://en.wikipedia.org/wiki/The_Tipping_Point_(book)

2. http://en.wikipedia.org/wiki/IPhone

3. http://news.cnet.com/8301-1023_3-10312804-93.html?tag=nl.e703

4. www.well.com/

5. www.loundy.com/CASES/Playboy_v_Hardenburgh.html

6. www.ibiblio.org/pub/academic/communications/logs/

7. http://en.wikipedia.org/wiki/Wikipedia:Vandalism

8. www.timesonline.co.uk/tol/news/uk/article1401041.ece

9. www.wifeinthenorth.com/2007/02/blog-to-book-in-60-seconds.html

10. http://wikimediafoundation.org/wiki/AppealCH/uk?utm_source=
    2009_Jimmy_Appeal1&utm_medium=sitenotice&utm_campaign=fundraiser
    2009&target=Appeal2

11. http://en.wikipedia.org/wiki/Craigslist_controversies_and_illegal_activities_
    by_users

12. http://en.wikipedia.org/wiki/Craigslist

13. http://snopes.com/photos/risque/kettle.asp

14. www.jennyhow.com/16-more-ebay-reflectoporn-pictures/

15. http://en.wikipedia.org/wiki/EBay_Haunted_Painting

16. www.dailymail.co.uk/sciencetech/article-1195651/How-Michael-Jacksons-
    death-shut-Twitter-overwhelmed-Google-killed-Jeff-Goldblum.html

17. http://twitter.com/EthanZ/status/2333139296

18. www.danah.org/papers/TakenOutOfContext.pdf

19. http://shankman.com/be-careful-what-you-post/

20. www.thekeyinfluencer.com/channel/2009/01/16/twittersituation/

21. www.facebook.com/legal/copyright.php?noncopyright_notice=1

22. http://social-media-optimization.com/2006/09/air-force-says-no-to-myspace/

23. http://blogs.guardian.co.uk/businessinsight/archives/2005/09/01/branded.html and http://www.lawyersandsettlements.com/articles/00008/baby_formula.html

24. www.davecarrollmusic.com/ubg/song1/

25. http://en.community.dell.com/dell-blogs/b/direct2dell/archive/2009/06/11/delloutlet-surpasses-2-million-on-twitter.aspx

26. www.informationweek.com/news/hardware/desktop/showArticle.jhtml?articleID=217801030&subSection=E-Business

27. http://mashable.com/2009/08/04/espn-social-media/

28. www.ibm.com/blogs/zz/en/guidelines.html

29. www.intel.com/sites/sitewide/en_US/social-media.htm

30. www.bbc.co.uk/blogs/technology/2009/12/twitter_iran_and_uksnow.html

31. http://twitter.com/terms

32. www.facebook-log.com/intellectual-property.htm

33. www.copyright.gov/circs/circ34.pdf

34. http://consumerist.com/5150175/facebooks-new-terms-of-service-we-can-do-anything-we-want-with-your-content-forever

35. http://news.bbc.co.uk/2/hi/talking_point/1375175.stm

36. http://en.wikipedia.org/wiki/New_Coke

37. www.bevnet.com/news/2008/10-13-2008-pepsi_redesign.asp

38. http://gs.statcounter.com/#search_engine-US-daily-20090501-20091207

39. www.bing.com/community/blogs/search/archive/2009/07/01/bringing-a-bit-of-twitter-to-bing.aspx

40. http://disney.go.com/disneyinteractivestudios/product.html?platform=
wii&game=disneyepicmickey

41. http://en.wikipedia.org/wiki/Web_2.0

42. http://en.wikipedia.org/wiki/Six_degrees_of_separation

43. http://en.wikipedia.org/wiki/Small_world_experiment

44. http://news.bbc.co.uk/1/hi/england/oxfordshire/8458822.stm

45. www.businessinsider.com/2008/10/apple-s-steve-jobs-rushed-to-er-after-heart-
attack-says-cnn-citizen-journalist

46. www.youtube.com/watch?v=7FRwCs99DWg

47. www.youtube.com/symphony

48. http://elastictime.wordpress.com/2009/01/20/i-found-my-horn-on-youtube,
http://smithivanson.wordpress.com/2009/04/02/a-huge-virtual-team

49. www.youtube.com/watch?v=9QFvfHXkd2o

50. http://blogs.nasa.gov/cm/blog/NASA-CIO-Blog/posts/post_1244861198431.html

51. www.telegraph.co.uk/technology/facebook/6954696/Facebook-bra-colour-
status-update-craze-raising-breast-cancer-awareness.html

52. www.telegraph.co.uk/technology/facebook/6953689/Urgent-Facebook-blood-
appeal-saves-British-students-life-after-Mexico-fall.html

53. www.insidesocialgames.com/2009/12/22/zynga-world-food-programme-team-
up-to-fight-hunger/

54. http://forrester.typepad.com/groundswell/2010/01/conversationalists-get-onto-
the-ladder.html

INDEX

Twitter

se primarily for SM

x day

nd other valuable SM / Hotel contributors

↳ Respond 2xday

e D'base to develop SM story

1 x SM mailshot

Repeat / repurpose on blog- with extra content on blog

Promote SM workshops

Reconfigure workshops to focus on 'How" + Strategy